CHRISTI

20C

Golden Years
of
Barnsley

TRUE NORTH BOOKS
DEAN CLOUGH
HALIFAX
WEST YORKS
HX3 5AX
TEL. 01422 344344
WWW.NOSTALGIA-BOOKS.CO.UK

First published in Great Britain by:
True North Books, Dean Clough, Halifax HX3 5AX
1998

ISBN 1 900 463 87 3

© Copyright: True North Books

This book is published in association with:

Hayselden

Golden Years of Barnsley

Text	*Kevin McIlroy*
Text pages design	*Mandy Walker*
Photographs compiled by	*Phil Holland*
Cover design	*Mark Smith*
Business development	*Stuart Glenholmes*

Contents

Introduction

I was flattered when Phil Holland of *True North Books* asked me to write the introduction for this, their latest book on Barnsley. My life in Barnsley began when I was 18, arriving from Filey to take up a post as a projectionist for the three local Rank cinemas. It was the early 1950s, and my working life was spent showing feature films at the Princess, the Old Empire (later the Odeon) and the Alhambra. I have many happy memories of my time with the Rank organisation and I have much to thank them for, not least being my introduction to Ada, later Mrs Bulmer, my best and longest friend and the love of my life. In my spare time I developed an interest in still photography, taking pictures with a small *Coronet* camera and acquiring a fascination for the changes taking place in Barnsley that has remained with me all my life. When I was in my early 20s there were just two professional photographers in Barnsley - Mr Denton and Mr Roberts. My interest in photography led to me being known by Mr Denton and eventually to him offering me a part-time job which I did alongside my work in the cinema. By the mid 1960s I was working full time on a range of commercial, portrait and wedding assignments for Mr Denton, building up my skills and making contacts with local people which would serve me well in later years.

Ray Sabine was a well-known Freelance Press Photographer in Barnsley. All the national newspapers used his work and when his business began to grow Mr Sabine asked me to join his staff. I had six happy years there which lasted until the end of the 1960s when I was offered a job as a photographer on the *Barnsley Chronicle*. Working on the 'Chronicle brought me into contact with thousands of local people, from Mayors to Football Stars and Chief Constables to ordinary people celebrating golden wedding anniversaries and 100th birthdays. I saw them all and enjoyed every minute of it. By the time I retired, in 1992, I had spent 26 years at the 'Chronicle - gone in the blink of an eye, and a privilege that I feel tremendously lucky to have enjoyed. A great love of my life is football. Becoming the official photographer for Barnsley Football Club in the late 1960s was an honour I will never forget.

Most people in Barnsley will be aware of our Photography business based at Old Mill Lane near the College. *Stan plus Stan Two* was established in 1978 by me and my son ('Stan Two' as our Bank Manager once remarked, unwittingly giving us the idea for the name of our business) and is now run virtually entirely by my very talented son. These days we do work for government departments and international companies - though we still have a loyal following of wedding and portrait clients to keep us busy and 'local.' My semi-retirement has given me more time to pursue my interest in local history and historic local photographs. One outlet for this is the talks I present to various groups around Barnsley at which I show slides taken from marvellous old photographs in my collection. Local people often call at the shop and donate their own old pictures to add to the collection, safe in the knowledge that they will be shown to a wider audience of Barnsley enthusiasts as I do my rounds on the 'talks' circuit. Here is a fitting place to express my gratitude for their kindness.

This book concentrates on the changes which have taken place in Barnsley over a period of around half a century and is bound to bring back memories of the way we used to live. The pages prove that the town has seen a great many changes. But I always say that it is 'people' who make a town, and Barnsley has the best you can get when it comes to this most important asset. I have adopted *Barnsley;* it is the place I have spent my best and most enjoyable years. Even more important than this, I have always felt that the people of Barnsley have adopted *me,* and I hope that helping to produce this book will be seen as something of a 'thank you' to the people of the town in return. I hope you enjoy it!

Stan Bulmer

Acknowledgments

The publishers would like to thank

Stan & Ada Bulmer

Wendy Hawkins

Local Studies section of Barnsley Central Library

Stan + Stan 2

Market Hill in the mid 1950s

Around the town centre

Left: The striking building in the centre of this photograph was constructed in the 1930s and was occupied, at this time, by Burton's, the tailors.
To the right was the Imperial Hotel, a very ornate edifice built in 1905 and demolished in 1957, to be replaced by shop units. In the foreground of the picture are Peel Square's underground conveniences.

Below: Two and four wheeled and pedestrian traffic does not have the stress we are used to today as we view Queen Street and the bottom of Market Hill. If shopping were ever a pleasure, then a stroll in this area on this Spring day would not be so unpleasant.
Crossing the road from Burtons at the Eldon Street corner to Market Hill or standing in the road putting the world to rights outside Yorkshire Penny Bank is almost a relaxation and if the street does become too busy then there is the Belisha beacon which will act as a magic carpet and transport you across. In the corner is Harralls on this site since 1912. Next door is Farm Stores, another survivor until 1973. Goodsons will eventually give way to Barnett and Hutton, fashion shop and Marks and Spencer, a 'must' in any town centre, has yet to expand next door to take over from Norwood's Opticians. Tailoring shops, Weaver to Wearer and Alexandre, are two more businesses to have established themselves in this part of Queen Street for a few years at least.

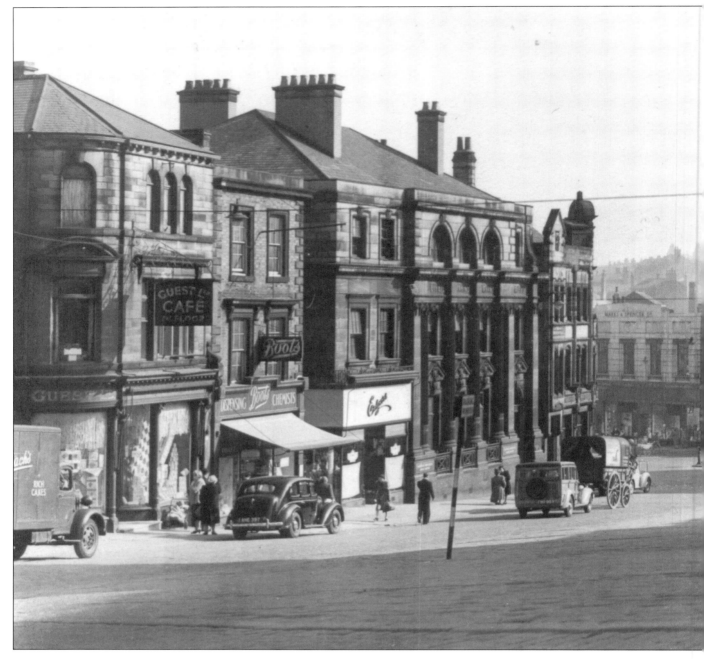

Above: A 1955 view of Market Hill and next to the entrance to Royal Street Arcade is Guest's cafe a long established family business here. The Arcade was established in 1893 when buildings were demolished to make a passage from Guest's yard to Market Hill. Today it is a good example of what can be done to keep alive a part of the town's history.

Next door is Boots the Chemist, not a local business, but being here since 1923 has given it some kind of residential status rather like the Midland Bank opposite. The leather goods shop of Spiers was another small firm to establish itself here before it had to give way to the march of commercial progress. Two banks take us to the corner of Eldon Street, one housing the old Yorkshire Penny Bank. Across the road from Guests to where at one time there used to be a small market is Cheesman's Printers with its van parked outside and what could be its driver taking the air. A picture to bring back some memories - you can almost smell Guest's roast coffee beans from here.

Right: The spire of Regent Street Congregational Church has a dignity of its own in comparison to Shambles Street in 1960 as we look towards what will be the site of the new library. But this is the age of re-development and reaction to a lot that passed as such was summed up by contemporary American singer, Joni Mitchell, when she sang 'They paved paradise and put up a parking lot.' Shambles Street was not paradise and no car park replaced it but the sentiment may well be valid here. There was a need to change. It is estimated that the car population increased by 400 percent between 1957 and 1970 and towns had to cope with this. Buildings as in Shambles Street were showing their age. People's shopping habits altered. Town centres were forced to take the strain and local authorities were urged by the government to 'save every acre'. So we saw in every town vast areas of land being cleared and shops and businesses replaced. What were concerns were the apparent necessity to remove buildings that were part of the town's heritage and the kind of replacements that were put in their place.

Bottom: Try looking at this 1924 photograph of the junction of Queen Street and Eldon Street looking towards May Day Green. Then put today's businesses in their place as well as remembering what replaced the old ones in the interim when the corner itself and the opposite side were transformed in 1930, Montague Burton with its unique frontage was erected to monopolise that corner. On the other side of Queen Street Marks and Spencer arrived in 1937 where The White Swan Inn stood. The building work has begun on the premises of the then Yorkshire Penny Bank, a structure which dominated that end of Eldon Street at the bottom of Market Hill. Today it sadly stands empty. The street on which stood shops that were part of Barnsley's life in the 1920s which housed local businesses like Goodson's Mantles now has businesses which are equally as part of the life of this town and in many cases that of many others.

Right: This is a view of Queen Street in 1924 looking towards Market Hill and there are some shops and businesses here which are famous in the recorded history of the town's commercial life. The Royal Oak Yard, the Maypole and Jacksons 3/9, the Hatters, became the site for Woolworth's original store with its sloping floor. Gaunts the jewellers was in the hands of Percy's father before he took on

the business. Evans, a hat shop, stood next to the Royal Oak, itself previously called the White Swan. Later Liptons became Melias and then Weaver to Wearer after that shop had moved next door from its first home. Crow, the butcher, and Black Boy Shoes are part of the original site of Marks and Spencer and next door Madame Shaw's Millinery shop eventually in 1973 turns into Slendos Gowns. Towns develop as needs and habits change and this quiet scene over seventy years ago reminds us how much Barnsley has changed to meet the demands of the time.

The large object in the foreground of the picture, which the workmen are looking at suspiciously, is a concrete lamp post, and it is presumably destined to be inserted into a hole somewhere off the left edge of the picture. The man in the shirtsleeves, tie and braces, probably one of the gaffers, appears to be measuring it to make sure that it will fit. History tells us that it did fit, and concrete lamp posts began to illuminate Barnsley in 1954, the year in which this photograph was taken. The site of this particular concrete lamp post is Market Hill, and we are looking up towards the Town Hall.

On the right Butterfields and Massies is holding a sale, so any ladies thinking about making themselves a new outfit will no doubt need to pop in to see what bargains are to be had, and perhaps to treat themselves to a little something at Butterfields cafe at the same time. Butterfields and Massies was one of Barnsley's long-established family businesses, having traded there since the 1830s. Further up the hill is the Royal Hotel, and beyond that, partially hidden by a large vehicle, is the handsome and easily-recognisable frontage of the Barnsley Permanent Building Society, which sits proudly on the corner of Regent Street with its fine pillared doorway set at an angle to the road.

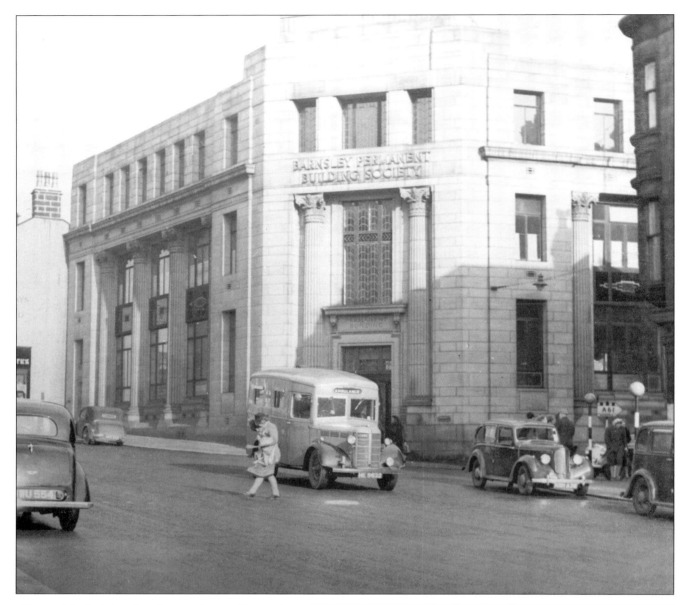

Above: No double yellow lines and no traffic wardens makes parking in Church Street in 1950 a stress-free activity. This street contains many fine buildings none more so than at its junction with Regent Street the headquarters of the Barnsley Permanent Building Society. This building, in style very much in keeping with the Town Hall further up the hill, was opened in 1936. On the other side of the junction can just be made out the older, but just as distinguished, branch of the then National Provincial Bank. When it opened in 1875 it was the London and Yorkshire Bank and is now the Royal Bank of Scotland. It would be interesting to try to recall the names of banks that were once features of every high street and have either closed, merged or disappeared. Think of the District bank, Martins, Westminster - they are the easy ones! No such difficulty with the bank beyond the building Society. The only thing that Barclays changed, apart from swallowing up one of the above 3, was to open another branch in Queen Street to supplement its Church Street branch where it had been since 1916. A fine street which, as it is said in another context, 'has kept its shape'.

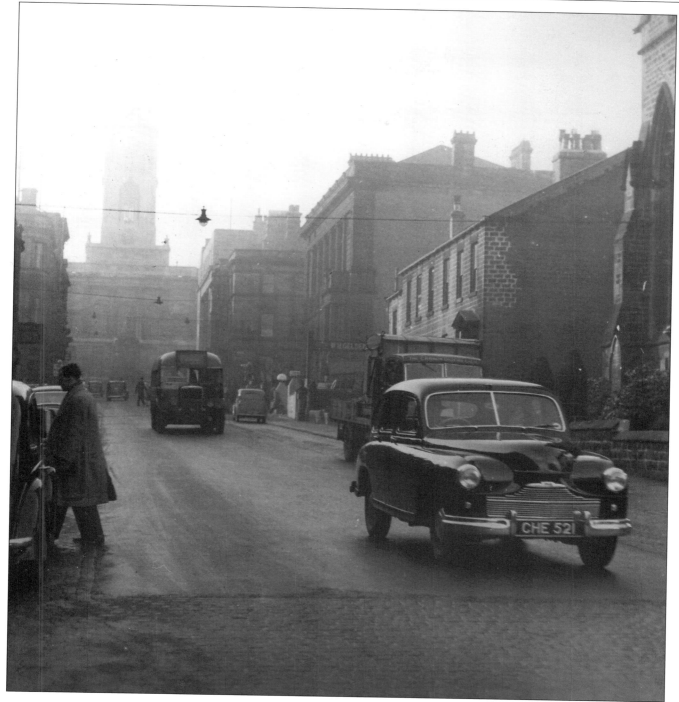

Facing page, bottom: This is a 1955 photograph of the passage between Liptons and the Imperial Hotel in Peel Square. The square still retains some of the buildings that made it such an impressive site although not necessarily performing the same function. The Imperial Hotel itself did not last beyond 1959 and is now home to a record store, while Liptons, here since 1925 expanded in 1961 to include the next door premises belonging to Cornan's Tobacconists and stayed until 1968. The yard itself still remains although the first floor of the Builders Exchange on its left is empty. The most impressive building here overlooks the Square where Pitt Street meets Wellington Street. Now a pub bearing the name of a one time Barnsley AFC mascot, it was once the home of the Barnsley Chronicle before the newspaper moved to Church Street in 1930. York County Bank in 1957 then became the latest in a series of businesses to occupy it, before the TSB took over and now it is the pub.

Above: Looking up Regent Street, with the Town Hall clock disappearing into the mist on this occasion, this is the view which must have greeted many a traveller to Barnsley as they emerged from the station at the bottom of the hill; the Town Hall is ideally positioned to welcome visitors to the town. The arched windows just visible to the right-hand edge of the photograph belong to the Regent Street Congregational Church, which was erected in 1856. The building next to the Church used to be a doctor's house and became the offices of the Britannic Assurance Company in 1946.
The car with the split windscreen which is coming down Regent Street has a typical Barnsley registration plate, CHE 521; vehicles first registered in Barnsley were very often allocated the letters HE.

The view that says 'This is Barnsley'. The Town Hall and the Technical and Mining College stand in line at the top of the hill. An occasional visitor to any town takes away usually one memory of it. In the case of Barnsley it is this Town Hall. This photograph was taken possibly in the late 1950s when there is life about Market Hill, not, as it sometimes appears today, of just traffic worming its way toward Shambles Street. The market stalls, the vans, the parked cars and the crowds they attracted were central to the life of the street and the

businesses like Harts, Woodhouse Currys, the Midland Bank, Zuckers and Goodworths, having been there for some time, give it its own kind of permanence. The building at the corner of Market Hill and Shambles Street was once the site of the Corn Exchange which burnt down in 1927. The policeman overseeing the zebra crossing would be a familiar figure with his own kind of authority here long before traffic wardens and pelican crossings, although there is someone sneaking across the road behind his back.

Above: At the height of cinema going Barnsley could boast it had eight or nine cinemas, the Alhambra Odeon, the nearby Star, or Big Hut, the Gaumont, the Globe, the Cosy on Pitt Street, the Empire Super Cinema and the three in this Town End part of the town, the Princess on Racecommon Road, the Ritz opposite Taylor's Mill on Peel Street and the Pavilion here at the Town End junction. Lives were governed by what we watched at the cinema almost as if it was the old equivalent of a modern soap opera and suddenly it all stopped. There came other things to compete for our money and more importantly our time. Television, sport, craft activities, clubs, bingo arrived in force and the cinema suffered. That which had been part of our culture with its Hollywood productions, British and American stars, legends to us all, and - just as important to many contemporary recollections - 'two-pennorth of darkness on the back row' was now just another form of entertainment and an expensive one too.

Below: Westgate, once the home at various stages of history of the Fire, Ambulance and Police stations, the Empire Palace, St Mary's Boys' School, The Tithe Barn, The Courts and Barnsley Boys Club, is now a hotch potch of a car park, a large office block, a new Police station on Churchfields, the Courts and what was once the Boys club. The area around Westgate was at one time a mix of yards in which were situated cramped dwelling houses. The Empire Palace, opposite the old Police Station and originally known as the Surrey Music Hall, lost its licence in 1908 and was turned into a warehouse, until it was demolished in 1954. The school building disappeared thirty years ago and the Fire and Ambulance stations are now on Broadway. The timber framed Tithe Barn, part used as a butcher's shop, was allowed to fall into disrepair and in 1968 the town eventually lost a valuable piece of its history. The old premises of the Boys Club only serves as reminder of what it was only by the name on the outside. The rest is not the building it was!

Charlie Chaplin became household names and an eight year old called Jackie Cooper, star of the 1932 film 'Sooky', was earning £500 per week. Whatever happened to him? We know what happened to the Pavilion - it was unfortunately burnt to the ground in September 1950. Town End had lost a symbolic landmark in the same way as it did when the Ritz was closed in 1974 and replaced by structures more in keeping with the times.

Top: The Gaumont cinema was opened on Eldon Street in 1956 at the height of the popularity of cinema going. The front doors of the cinema were from the old Empire Cinema which had been gutted by fire two years earlier. Like all new cinemas at the time it was extremely well-equipped with facilities for Cinemascope, the successor to 3D films and those spectacles you had to wear to see properly and which often could be a nuisance! This really was the age of cinema going. Television was confined to the few and the choice of programmes was limited. Bingo was still called Housey Housey so the Alhambras and the Gaumonts could often announce 'Only seats at the front'. The films that were most popular in those great days were 'Bridge on the River Kwai', 'Breakfast at Tiffanys' starring the lovely Audrey Hepburn, who proved in the film she was a better actress than a singer, and 'Pyscho' with that awful murder scene in the shower. But times change, cinema-going falls out of fashion and Bingo soon takes over.

Above: The popular Pavilion Cinema at Town End started out in life in 1909 as the Olympia Roller Skating Rink with a cafe and resident expert skaters before it became a cinema in 1920. At the time the Pavilion was opened, there were over three thousand cinemas in the country. These were the days of 'mood' music as the pianist tried to accompany the action. The musicians were highly talented people and when 'talkies' arrived in 1929, many went on to other parts of the musical world to demonstrate their talents. Colour films arrived in the 1930s and Sunday showings were allowed after 1932. Cinema going was part of the national culture and half of those attending were children and young people and, of the rest, three-quarters were women. So Gary Cooper, Tom Mix and

Golden years of BARNSLEY

Below: Looking down Church Street towards Market Hill, the railings round the War Memorial which stands in front of the Town Hall can be seen on the right, with the base of the Memorial going off the edge of the picture; the Town Hall itself is set back from here.

Half-way down the hill on the left is the Royal Hotel. The Royal Hotel used to be called the White Bear, but it changed its name, so the story goes, after Princess Victoria and the Duchess of Kent stopped there with their entourage for refreshments and a change of horses in 1835. As the White Bear, this establishment had in any case been prone to confusion with another nearby inn named the Old White Bear.

The building with the arched windows just above the Royal Hotel had housed a banking establishment since 1875; on this photograph, it is the National Provincial Bank, which has been there since 1924.

Right: The experience of having your photograph taken was obviously a new one for this postman from the nearby Regent Street office standing on Church Street in the late 1920s outside Arthur Wright's Chemists shop. The other postman seems more interested in his work or avoiding the pedal cyclist, however. Behind is the Royal Hotel, formerly a coaching inn from where the mail set off for London.

On the opposite side of the road were businesses like Maudsley the Bootmaker, Griffiths Printing Works, and Shoesmith's Grocery shop. At the corner with Regent Street was Dr Sadler's House, the site of which will became the headquarters of the Barnsley Permanent Building Society.

The west side of Church Street will at this time be widened, the buildings demolished and there will soon be the Town Hall and the Technical College. It needs more than a second glance to match this view of Church Street with the way it is today.

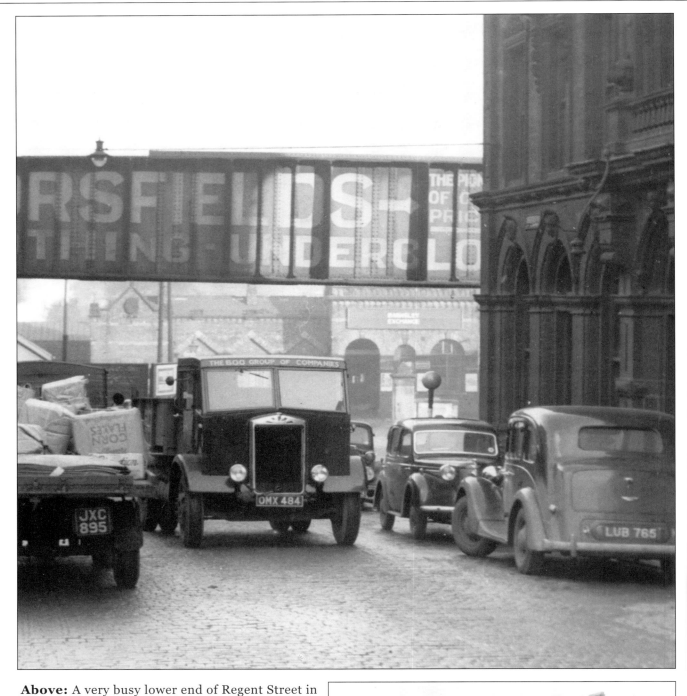

Above: A very busy lower end of Regent Street in February 1950 with the iron span of the railway bridge carrying an advertisement for one of the town's more famous shops.

The Court House Station, now sadly closed to anything, to the left would be in 1950 at its busiest. That bridge has gone now, demolished in 1961 but there is still evidence of its existence with the wall and pillar to be seen. The reason why the Court House Station closed was that the railway bridge which crossed Elton Road was going to cost so much to repair, it was cheaper to close the station and move to Exchange Station nearby. Across the road from the Court House is the imposing front of the Queen's Hotel. Opened in 1885 it was, like many other hotels built at the time, designed to serve the rail travelling public as passenger numbers increased due to the rapid expansion of the system.

Facing page, bottom: Among the dust and the rubble of Sheffield Road stands the imposing facade of the Alhambra Odeon cinema. It had opened on 1st October 1915 as a theatre with seating for two thousand six hundred people. Quite surprising for at the time the country did have other things on its mind. The theatre did have the frontage of a late Edwardian Theatre very much in the style of similar establishments built in other northern towns at the turn of the century. The glittering opening night was devoted to raising funds for the Soldiers' and Sailors' Help Society in the form of a concert.

The revues and shows continued until the theatre, under pressure from 2 other local theatres, the Theatre Royal and the Empire, decided to take advantage of the growing popularity of the film and became a cinema.

The dispensary at the corner of Peel Street has now given way to a fast food store and entertainment shop

Above: A good view up Shambles Street from Town End. The Dispensary at the corner with Peel Street has given way to a fast food store and an instant entertainment shop. The Barnsley Canister Company here stands in front of Britton's Accountants on the opposite corner. Now that building has been renovated and re-named the Linen Court, the only apparent reminder of the many Town End linen establishments. Round the corner on Summer Lane was Sparrow Park or Town End Park which led to Fitzwilliam Street. The Pinfold Steps lead up to the old Primitive Methodist Chapel, then the new home of the Barnsley Boys Club. This area was once a centre of business and industry and entertainment and also was almost a village, or at least its own community, as well being the entrance to the town from all the converging roads. Hard to imagine from this 1960s photograph that it ever lived up to that description.

A lone see-saw and a just as solitary car stand in the middle of what were the side streets around Heelis Street whose houses were demolished in the clearances years earlier. These patches here in 1967 are just play areas now and during this clearing process there was a rock which was too large to be moved so it stayed put, no doubt acting as another addition to the play amenities of the local children. As a result of the removal of those cramped streets and equally as cramped houses, we are given the opportunity to look at

Barnsley town centre from another angle. Start nearer to Heelis Street. Behind Veal's Printers in this picture is Taskers, photographer and archivist of the town's past. 'Island Corner', the home of the Barnsley Co-op with its distinctive chimney and clock tower, is a definite landmark and behind is the Town Hall with the Court House to the rear and beside it the Technical College with the Regent Street Congregational Church, now, sadly, missing from the town's landscape, completing a real roof-top tour of the town.

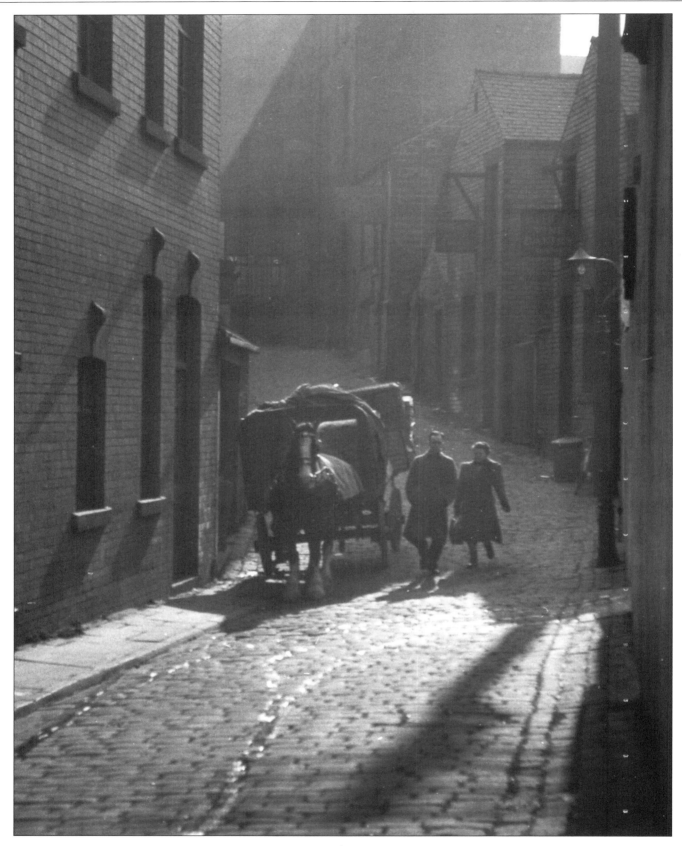

As you look at this photograph, you can almost hear the clip-clop of the horse's iron shoes on the cobbles and the rattling and creaking of the cartwheels over the uneven surface.

This atmospheric snapshot was taken in Hayes Croft, a little turning off New Street. Hayes Croft used to be home to tradesmen such as Jimmy Croft the signwriter and the Vine Bakery.

The street still exists, behind Boots in the town centre, but redevelopment works which have included the construction of the new Alhambra Shopping Centre have changed the little backstreets in this part of town almost beyond recognition; some of the buildings in this photograph have been cleared, and Hayes Croft is now a service road for the modern shops at the end.

Above: Ladies, possibly from the nearby CEAG factory, pass the old premises of the Electricity Board. At the end of the last century the Government had allowed municipal authorities to establish their own power supplies which they could sell for commercial and business use and it was not until the nationalisation process of the post-war government that this became a centralised service. Round the corner from the bottom of Midland Street was Gas Nook where appropriately Gas premises were sited. Here the Electricity offices are empty, prior to the

development of another showroom and offices. Soon this whole area will change as the need to redevelop the housing, transport and shopping areas of the town to meet the changing needs of the time becomes more essential. In 1969 later than in other northern towns came the planners and the developers and these changes began. What is of contention is what form the changes took!

Top: The old Post Office sign on the right of Regent Street shows where Barnsley's main Post Office used to be situated. Many generations would have patiently queued here for postage stamps, postal orders and family allowances, to send a telegram, and all the other services which the General Post Office offered in this building between 1882 and 1967. Originally it was a two-storey building, and the third floor was added later. The Barnsley Permanent Building Society headquarters, on the corner on the left behind the bus, were opened in 1936. Further down Regent Street, the Gothic spire rising high above the surrounding buildings is that of Regent Street Congregational Church, which was demolished in 1971. The styling of the cars and the single-decker bus coming up Regent Street from the direction of the station give an indication as to the date of this photograph, which was in fact taken in 1950.

This fine panoramic view of the area around the Cross Keys Hotel was created using the simple but effective technique of joining together two photographs, taken one immediately after the other. The scaffolding which has crept into the bottom left corner of the picture tells us that changes are afoot in this part of town, where the fish market used to be, and the tower crane, top right behind the buildings, tells us something about the magnitude of these changes. On the left, the building with the scalloped roof survived the redevel-

opment, as did Woolworth's next door, but the Cross Keys Hotel did not. Within two years of this photograph, the Cross Keys had been demolished. It had stood here since the time of Queen Victoria, and had pulled many a pint of Barnsley Bitter for thirsty shoppers and traders. H Samuel, the well-known jewellers, had opened their shop in the building on the left in 1962; previous occupants of the building had included a tailors and Hunters Tea Store. Next door to H Samuel is Paige, the ladies outfitters.

Above: Barnsley Court House Station in Regent Street had been closed as a station since 1960 and here in 1967 is home to a drapery shop. It had been built as a court house in 1861 and as the railway system expanded a better use was found for it and it became Barnsley's main station in 1870, replacing the original Barnsley Station at Cudworth. Although Barnsley was never destined to be part of the north-south main line system, or the diversion to Sheffield, it did provide more than useful link with the rest of west and south Yorkshire, east to Hull and west to Manchester and beyond. The 'parochial' nature of the service helped to give it an affection only local trains can inspire. Remember the 'Cudworth Flyer', anything but, or the other stations on your journey when you stopped at stations like Penistone, Monk Bretton, Birdwell and Hoyland, Cudworth itself and the noise of banging of doors, gushes of grey steam, powerful men with green and red flags, sometimes unexplained and interminable waits, wondering if the train would ever get there - the golden age of steam. The Court House Station was modernised in 1955 when it was given new canopies but by the time it closed, it was only taking the Barnsley to Sheffield line and a few parcel trains.

Above right: By 1964 Shambles Street looked a sorry sight as shops were left abandoned, areas of cleared land became temporary patched-up car parks and eventually replacement shops and offices were constructed. Shops which had become features of life here were gone. Green's

Radio, Don Valley Cleaners, Robinson's locksmiths, Blenkinsop's butchers became memories and were replaced by British Relay, Watson's Tobacconists and Les White's Menswear. Of all the public houses which served this once main thoroughfare only the 'Three Travellers', now bearing another name, at the corner of Dog Lane, has survived as the drinking habits and the social lives of the nation began to change. The old style pubs either closed or were re-fashioned to meet the demands for more pleasant surroundings. There was an increase in the number of female customers and new beers and new drinks were introduced. It was expected that food would now be served. So the pub's image, its clientele and its function underwent this change, especially as there were too many of them in such an area as Shambles Street at that time and other places began to provide stiff competition for people's custom.

The Sheffield Road flats and St John's Church at the corner of Joseph Street and Wood Street overlook this view of Sheffield Road and it is a local firm which dominates the photograph. Wigfalls came into its own in the days of 'You've never had it so good' as explained to us by the Prime Minister in the 1960s, Harold McMillan. This was the time of a rise in consumer spending and electrical items such as refrigerators, washing machines and colour televisions, which today are regarded as commonplace in the home, *were then things to be saved up for and acquired. Even smaller items came more into their own like transistor radios and hair dryers and so Wigfalls, taking advantage of this need and able to offer hire purchase in the form of easy payments or rental in the case of televisions, prospered and expanded. But like a lot of other successful local businesses it was swallowed up by the national chains and the idea of supporting local firms began to fade as the opportunity was increasingly denied.*

A bird's-eye view of Market Hill shows the crane in the background which was bringing change to the other side of Barnsley, but so far Market Hill has escaped the attention of the developers. The Town Hall is off the bottom of the picture, but the paved area around the War Memorial in front of it is visible, with the seats where weary shoppers could pause for a rest as they struggle up the hill with heavy shopping bags. The market is open, and a mobile shop selling home-made bread and cakes is parked just round the corner from Shambles Street, outside the Halifax Building Society. Vans such as this used to travel their routes round Barnsley, selling fresh produce door-to-door; housewives would know when to expect the breadman, and the fishman, and the vegetable man, and would listen out for toot of the van out in the street which heralded their arrival. Opposite the bread van is W H Smith, with Castles furniture store next door down the hill; carrying on down, we emerge opposite Marks and Spencer.

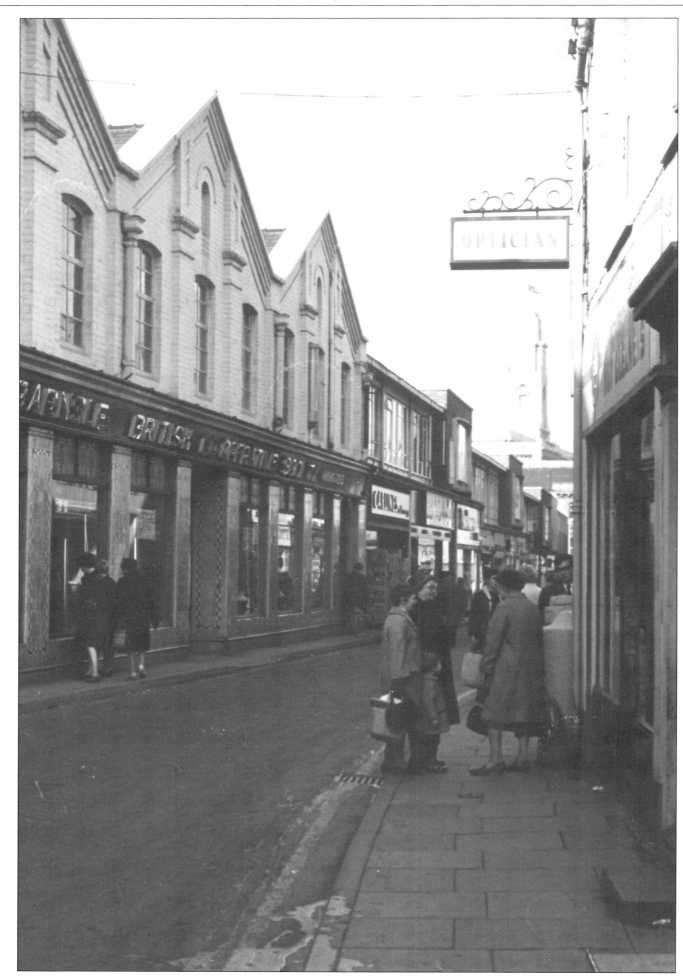

Left: You never needed to take a watch with you when you went shopping in Barnsley, because the Town Hall clock, with a face on each side, was visible from almost everywhere in town. Here, looking up at the clock from Market Street, we have the Barnsley British Co-operative Society building stretching along the street on our left, long enough for its full name to be displayed along its length. The building used to belong to Vero's Printing Works, who had a shop in Queen's Street. And anyone who finds the Town Hall clock difficult to see might want to visit Dolland and Aitchison, the optician whose sign can be seen on the right. Dolland and Aitchison moved into these premises in 1962.

Below left: At the end of this parade of shops at the bottom of Market Hill is the old Curry's, which had a bicycle showroom upstairs. During the 50s many towns had a Curry's, which sold electrical goods as well as cycles and accessories. Next door to Curry's is Butcher's bakers and confectioners. Many people considered this the best bread shop in Barnsley; Butcher's had the shop between 1932 and 1966, and it then became Goodworth's, whose bread and cakes were just as popular. Moving up the hill, Harts, the decorating merchants, was a very long-established business, having occupied these premises since 1835; Woodhouse was a furniture store, which had been here since 1936. Their building subsequently became a bingo hall called Cossiboat Bingo. Note the television aerials which are beginning to appear on chimneys.

Bottom: Some of the shops which can be seen in Sheffield Road in this picture have a very long history. On the left Horsfields, the 'pop' shop at numbers 59 to 63 Sheffield Road, could trace its origins back to at least the 1880s. As well as pawnbroking services, Horsfields sold boots, shoes, outfitting and bedding. A specially-made clock with Horsfields name on hung outside. Horsfields Bargain Shop was well-known in Barnsley, particularly amongst those who found it difficult to make the weekly wage packet last the week, but closed down in 1971. Beyond Horsfields is Castles Furniture Shop, which was established in 1846, and Coombes Footwear, who began trading in 1897, moved into this area in 1931, and continued to sell quality boots and shoes here until they closed down in 1967.

Above: The shops at the end of Cheapside look as bleak as the weather with the sole pair of shoppers appearing to look for a shop that is still open. From this photograph it is hard to imagine that Cheapside, with Eldon Street, was one of the principal shopping streets of the town as well as being the longest established. But it is the time of change not just for the shops but for the people who lived and worked there. At this busy junction traffic generally had its own policeman directing it and on cold damp days like this who could blame him not welcoming a cup of hot tea from any meat trader with a stall nearby? Soon Peter Pell, men's tailors, which can be made out at the corner of New Street, will eventually become a branch of John Collier, 'The Window to Watch' and this whole area over a period of three years will be transformed in an attempt to maintain its reputation as the place to shop.

Above right: An empty fish market opposite the May Day Green Market with names of stall holders to recall. Shoppers could reach the market from Kendray Street or down the steps from Eldon Street. Edward's stall seems to be the odd one out as his speciality was fruit and vegetables. The slabs are bare at Coe's and Rusby's, which once had Wainwright as part of the firm, and at the other long standing traders. Zucker's stands in the corner beside Wilson's dress shop and to the rear of the advertising hoardings is the Cross Keys Hotel. This hotel was demolished in 1972 and one interesting fact is that it had the same landlord, Mr James Cressey, from 1924 to 1960. Out of picture here was the Public Weigh House which stood next to the Cross Keys which had a bell on top which was rung to signal the end of the market. And the permanent end of this market it was soon to be to make way for the new shopping centre and a re-designed market area.

Looking down Sheffield Road into town, we must admire the spirit of the ecclesiastical building which sits bravely between a pub and a cinema. The Alhambra was built here in 1915. During the First World War it was a theatre with seating for 2,600. It became a cinema by 1926, and would have showed silent films to the accompaniment of live keyboard music before the talkies came in. In the photograph, taken in 1956, the sign reads Odeon Alhambra; the Alhambra became part of the Odeon chain of cinemas in the 1950s. Unfortunately this cinema gave up the battle to attract audiences relatively early, and screened its last feature film in November 1960. But if cinemas were finding it difficult to pull people in at that time, bingo halls encountered no such problems, and in 1962 the premises were given a new lease of life as the Vale Bingo Club. This lasted for a decade or so, when once again falling numbers led to closure. This time there was no reprieve; the building was left standing empty for another decade or so, at the end of which time, having failed to find a purchaser, it was demolished.

The Sheffield Road, Cheapside area looking up New Street at the site of the soon to be built Alhambra Centre. The near side of the road is being cleared to make way for road widening, Hardy's furnishing shop was situated here between 1965 and 1967 and eventually Dolcis shoes occupied the premises. This was the age of the consumer and goods like washing machines, once regarded as a luxury, were now an essential item in every home. Each house was beginning at this time to acquire its share of other 'labour saving devices' so freeing the housewife - and her husband - from the drudgery of housework and giving more time for leisure pursuits. The advancement of the technology in television, the introduction of colour and the advent of new channels made television viewing a national way of life. Consequently there came the increase in sales of sets and, with the growth of the hire purchase industry and other rental schemes, it allowed firms like DER to prosper.

Above: A view of Town End looking up Summer Lane and the traffic where six main roads meet is already in the 1960s showing the strain the junction was under and which necessitated later the building of the Western Relief Road. This may have gone some way to solving the problem of dealing with the great rise in the number of commercial and private vehicles using this part of the town. Just as probably, however, it has removed the sense of township that this part of Barnsley possessed as a roundabout has cut a swathe through the junction and caused each road to be separate units rather than part of a community. The shops and the public houses which were an integral part of the junction have disappeared or have altered in status - buildings like the Race Street baths still stand with the

distinctive chimney intact but serve another useful purpose now as Town End performs another vital function in the life of the town more in keeping with the needs of the 1990s.

Above right: Another view of Town End prior to its dramatic change in appearance. The post office traditionally at the corner of Racecommon Road and York Street lasted until 1967. The area was once the centre of Barnsley's famous linen industry and at a time when the industrial towns of the north try for educational reasons at least to keep within their memory bank associations with their industrial past, there is little in the area today which suggests as such. If nothing else the area had some of the more well known public houses of the town including, the Fitzwilliam, the Locke Park Hotel which closed in 1965 and at the corner of Dodworth Road and Racecommon Road the Wheatsheaf, the closure of which in 1990 was the subject of a fierce debate but like much else of the area it had to give way to the construction of the new relief road.

Sporting life

Above: In the season when local heroes Barnsley AFC were relegated to the Third Division North with the worst ever record in the club's history, the Doncaster Road school football team can show off their trophy as League Champions in 1952/3 and the line-up is:- Mr F Taylor (games master), Mr A H Park (Headteacher). Back; Len Barraclough, Peter Patterson, Geoff Moxon. Middle; Fred Nicholls, Barry Farmer, Keith Bennett. Front; Maurice Clark, Edgar Dyson, Clem Wood, Gary Simpson, John McFarland Certainly it is a proud moment for those boys and they look very smart too. Older ones among us will remember the kind of boots we wore in those days and the ball that was sometimes too heavy to kick. Heading it was no pleasure either. But that didn't matter when you have won a trophy with your school-mates and the only school league tables that were important then were primary school football ones.

Both pages: Four photographs of the boys from the Barnsley Boys Club with their leaders and instructors. The Physical Training instructor for the boys from 1946 to 1953 was George Joseph Brayfield, better known to them and to everybody else as 'Adger'. The first headquarters of the club, founded in 1933, were in Nelson Street and a camp at Cayton Bay was one of the first real outside activities. The club had even then in those pre-war years a reputation not only for the activities it provided for the boys but also for the organisation and skills of the leaders and instructors and it became a model for other clubs and towns to follow. The boys were encouraged to take part in draughts and chess, table tennis, football and cricket and boxing. Crafts subjects were on offer in the workshop; they could take part in debates and dramatics; the club established a library, a canteen and a savings club. The news letter, entitled 'The Harlequin', became a regular feature. This is why it was held in such high esteem.

During the war the club could boast that like the Windmill Theatre in London, 'it never closed' and its leader then, Don 'Pot' Pierrepont who died in 1960, guided it through those times towards another landmark in the club's history when it moved to new premises, the old Primitive Methodist Chapel in Westgate. All through its time the club had to rely mainly on its own efforts to raise money. To acquire the funds to obtain these new premises took a great effort by all concerned with the club. It was grateful to people like the Yorkshire and England Cricket captain, Norman

Yardley, for their active support. The club went from strength to strength in its new home and in 1960 the new leader appointed to replace the stalwart Pierrepont was Roy Bellamy. Still money was hard to come by and the leader in 1974, Brian Chapman,

introduced like canoeing, orienteering and climbing, including the thrill of abseiling. The patron of the National Association of Boys Clubs, singer Frankie Vaughn, who spent so much time and energy supporting the movement, visited the club in 1983 for its Golden Anniversary and found a novel way of raising funds. At the ceremony in the Civic Hall to celebrate this unique achievement, during which he gave a short concert, he sold kisses to his many female admirers.

It is estimated that during its life the Barnsley Boys Club had over fifteen thousand members on its books and its story chronicles a remarkable achievement. If you think of these thousands of boys who benefited from the

undertook a sponsored run from Barnsley in Gloucestershire to South Yorkshire. The range of activities widened. On offer were the traditional activities including camps, as seen here at Grassington, and the displays of gymnastics in venues such as Cawthorne Park but new ones were

foresight of the original founders and backers, from the efforts of the dedicated leaders, of instructors like Brayfield and of the host of volunteer helpers, it is a great pity that the state today of its old Westgate premises does not reflect the service they gave to the club and the club gave to the town.

Top left: When you have dreamt all your life about playing for your home-town club and that dream comes true and then to be told that you should leave and transfer to another, it is understandable that your first response is that you do not want to go. But Tommy Taylor, who had signed as a teenager for Barnsley rather than Hull City from Smithies United, was a local lad and wanted to stay that way. He had attended Raley Secondary Modern School which had a reputation for encouraging sporting talent amongst its pupils, Tommy's first weekly wage packet contained £2 8s 1d. After doing his national service which made him a physically stronger player, he played his first senior game for the club during the 1952-3 season, After forty-four appearances with twenty-six goals for the club he loved so much, he was transferred to Manchester United, becoming the then most expensive player in England. Soon he gained his first international cap and became one of that famous Manchester team managed by Matt Busby that swept all before them in the 1950s and broke the Football Association's barriers by entering the newly established European Cup competition. So the player that was so proud of his own town club and regarded as the finest header of the ball in the country also became one of the most respected players in the game not only in England but also abroad and, as a team-mate at the time stated, he was a 'player's player and a great person'.

Bottom left:
Remembered for his desire to practise his skills at training with an actual football and receiving the reply from the manager to the effect it was not necessary as he would see enough of it on Saturday, Danny Blanchflower was regarded as one of the greatest players not only to play for Barnsley but also within the game itself. He had joined the club from Glentoran for £6,000 in 1949 and slightly built Blanchflower soon attracted the attention of other clubs. After only seventy appearances for Barnsley, the Northern Ireland International and later his country's captain left for Aston Villa and then moved to Scarborough-born Bill Nicholson's famous 'push and run' Tottenham Hotspur which became the first ever side to win the cup and league double. It seems odd that a player like Blanchflower, whose skill on the field made him almost a legend and who thought so

deeply about the game, should not have been as successful as a manager.

Top right: To be signed as a replacement for the great Stanley Matthews would be regarded as a tremendous tribute to your talent but when the great man had no thoughts of giving up and you had to play out of position it would be more than frustrating. That was the fate of Higham-born Arthur Kaye in that Blackpool team in the late-fifties. In 1958 after two hundred and eighty appearances for Barnsley and becoming the club's most popular player, he fell out with his home town club in a dispute over wages and had signed for the Seasiders. His loyalty to the Barnsley club did not receive the reward it deserved and the Under-23 international missed out on joining the then big time clubs and, most disappointingly of all, on a 1958 England World Cup place. The feeling at the time was by playing for a more fashionable club would have secured him that coveted place. On leaving Blackpool, Arthur joined Middlesbrough but it is at Barnsley where he is best remembered for his willingness to take on opposing defences and the power of his shooting.

Bottom right: In days when full-backs played at the back Barry Murphy was the most respected defender Barnsley had ever had on its books for many a year. A star he may not have been, but for endeavour, diligence and loyalty he was close to being one. Signed from North Eastern League team, South Shields, in 1962, he gained a regular place in the first team at the age of twenty-seven and went on to make a record one hundred and eighty-two consecutive appearances for the club. Dropped only once, his final tally in the red shirt was five hundred and sixty-seven - unlikely that will ever be bettered. Barry was not noted for his speed but for his defensive guile in closing down his man and sticking with him. He was the fans' player of the year in 1972 and retired from the game at the age of thirty-eight. His other claim to fame was he was Barnsley's first ever substitute, coming on against Doncaster Rovers in October 1965. In an age when to some players club loyalty is not so important, his example stands out and for that at least he earned everyone's respect.

Barnsley's first ever substitute (Barry Murphy) came on against Doncaster Rovers in October 1965

Above: The Barnsley team that took on Leeds United in September 1950 in a 2-all draw contained some of the most skillful players in the club's history in Blanchflower, Jimmy Kelly, McCormack and Baxter. In the two Kellys it had some of its greatest characters although the sight of Eddie McMorran seeming to physically terrorise opposing defences was the one that thrilled the crowds so much. 'Town' clubs like Barnsley, as opposed to big city clubs, often inspired the greatest loyalty in players, particularly in the days when clubs and players were a real part of the local community. A typical example was centre-half Gordon Pallister who joined the club at the age of twenty, played until he was well into his thirties and continued that association long past then.

The team line for the game was:- Back: Danny Blanchflower, Eddie Bannister, Pat Kelly, Dave Lindsay, Gordon Pallister, Arthur Glover. Front: Gavin Smith, Eddie McMorran, Cec McCormack, Jimmy Baxter, Johnny Kelly. Goalscorers on this day were Baxter and McCormack and the crowd was 37,633.

Above right: A pre-development view of Oakwell which would have been a familiar sight to the faithful supporters of Barnsley AFC long before the recent glory years, before the implementation of the Taylor report, before Premier Leagues and the all-seater stadium. This stand structure still remains although the seats now stretch to the touchline. but the press and the directors' areas are still in their original places and there is a television gantry instead of the club sign now. Supporters with very long memories will recall the days of hope after the Second World War when football was so popular and crowds flocked to see the resurgence of league football after the mix and match of the war years. Interestingly the war-time government was at pains during the 1939-45 period to ensure that competitive football was played. So with Angus Seed as manager and new players like George Robledo, Kelly, Baxter and Blanchflower, Barnsley football club set out in those post-war years to entertain and the roars of support from the large crowds were for a Barnsley team at last.

If there was one man who ever regretted in a footballing sense the coming of the Second World War it was Angus Seed, Barnsley Football Club's manager. Appointed to the post in 1937, after being in charge of Aldershot for ten years, Barnsley was at a bit of a low ebb, but he transformed it to such an extent that the team won promotion within two years, One reason for this success was his shrewd dealings in the transfer market, including buying his best purchase of all, Johnny Steele, without actually seeing him play. That final season the team scored ninety-four goals and conceded thirty-four and finished eleven points ahead of second placed Doncaster Rovers, However, just when it was expected that the team would do great things, league football was abandoned until the end of the war. Here we see we see him with his team at training in 1945 but six years is a long time in the life of football and unfortunately those great days for him and the club never came.

Scoring points

When motor mechanic Tom Hayselden set up in business in 1959, his goals were fairly modest. All he wanted was to be his own boss, and to make enough money to provide for his wife and baby son. With this aim firmly in mind, he managed to borrow enough money to buy his first premises, which consisted of a small garage with three petrol pumps and a piece of land, in Wath-upon-Dearne.

With hindsight, Tom's timing in starting his business was just right, but at the time it seemed a brave step to take. In the late 50s and early 60s, motor cars were, to most people, a luxury and not a necessity, and the mining communities of South Yorkshire could afford few luxuries. Consequently there was a very limited market for Tom's services. He had to work hard, and his first years in business were not without their difficulties; even in his wildest dreams he could scarcely have imagined, at that time, that within a few decades of starting out Hayselden would be the area's largest independently owned motor dealership, selling in excess of two thousand vehicles a year and employing around one hundred and eighty staff at six

Above: *Mike Hayselden in his glory. Winner takes all.*
Below: *A close up view of Mike Hayselden on the racing track in 1969.*

sites. The success of the business can be attributed to a number of factors, one of which is, of course, the tremendous growth of car ownership amongst the middle and working classes in the 1960s. Equally if not more important, however, are the hard work which Tom put into the business, and his commitment to maintaining the very highest standards of customer service and supplying only the best quality products. Tom's garage began to gain a reputation for good workmanship at a fair price, and, as car ownership increased, recommendations from satisfied customers brought him a steady flow of new clients from Barnsley's growing number of motorists. Tom's late wife Marjorie also played an important part in the early success of the business, with her tremendous drive and business acumen perfectly complementing Tom's technical skills.

Hayselden's association with Volkswagen began in 1961. Today, Volkswagen is one of the world's leading car manufacturers, but in those days the name Volkswagen, to most people, was synonymous with Beetle, Volkswagen's one popular best seller.

Tom Hayselden's decision to enter into a franchise with a manufacturer whose stake in the British car market was represented by a single 'niche' model brought no guarantee of success, but it was a decision which paid dividends in the years which followed, as the close links which developed between manufacturer and dealer confirmed that both parties shared the same ideals of quality, reliability and value for money. The association has continued to this day, to the mutual benefit of both companies; Hayselden now has two Volkswagen showrooms where Volkswagen's complete current range of class-leading vehicles is displayed, and has won awards for its performance in sales campaigns and its high standards of service.

At around this time Tom Hayselden was joined in building up the franchise by his son Mike, who had inherited his father's

Top: *Mike Hayselden beats Ian Douglas in the Supervee race at Silverstone in 1972.*
Above: *An early example of one of Barnsley football club's labels to stick in your car.*

love of cars and was also a keen sportsman, with a passion for football and motor racing. Having won every available trophy in kart racing as a sixteen year old, Mike graduated to saloon car racing in 1966. In his first Mini race, the competitors who passed the chequered flag behind him included a young man named James Hunt. Like James Hunt, Mike subsequently made the transition into single seaters, with the newly launched Formula Vee and Super Vee Series. After winning championships in 1970 and 1971, Mike faced a difficult decision: to pursue his career in motor racing to its full potential would require serious commitment in terms of both money and time, and this would almost certainly mean giving up his place in the family business. There can be no doubt that, had he decided to concentrate on

Above: *Ian Banks and Joe Joyce collecting new cars from Hayseldens in 1981.* ***Left:*** *An early example of one of their advertisements.*

Football Club at the age of six, when his uncle Jack had taken him to Oakwell to see Barnsley play Brighton and Hove Albion in the third round of the F A Cup on a freezing cold January day in 1953. As Barnsley fans will remember, it developed into a particularly exciting match, with Barnsley losing 0-3 at half time, but managing to rally in the second half to win 4-3. The occasion is imprinted vividly on Mike's memory, and he still has the programme as a souvenir. From then on, he was a devoted Barnsley supporter. Even though his home in Bolton-on-Dearne was more conveniently situated for travelling to watch one of the two Sheffield teams, and even though Barnsley were relegated to the third division at the end of that season, young Mike scarcely missed a match at

motor racing, he would have achieved great success; but he gave the sport up, a decision no doubt applauded by not only the motorists of Barnsley, but by James Hunt as well.

As one door closes, another opens, because whilst Mike's decision to devote himself to the family business meant giving up his motor racing activities, it brought him the opportunity to become more involved with his other great sporting passion, football. Mike had become a fan of Barnsley

Above: Norman Hunter receiving sponsored shirts.
Below: Barnsley F.C Chairman Mr G Buckle with Mike Hayselden.

Oakwell and followed the Club to as many away fixtures as he possibly could, and has remained loyal ever since. In 1977 an opportunity arose to mix business with pleasure when Hayselden became the main supplier of vehicles to the Club, and in 1981 the company not only supplied cars but also

sponsored the club strip. Supporters from that era will never forget the sight of football heros such as Glavin, Aylott, Parker and McCarthy, in the red Barnsley shirt with Hayselden emblazoned across the front, leading their team to victory. Hayselden was also the first local business to sponsor the

annual Player of the Year Award ceremony, and the ties between Hayselden and Barnsley Football Club were cemented in 1994 when Mike Hayselden achieved a long-cherished ambition when he became a director of the club, a position which he still holds today.

● *In the nick of time! Speight slides in to foil bound Striker Derrick Park*

DEN LTD.

It is entirely typical of the Hayselden ethos that, whilst its affiliation with Barnsley Football Club is no doubt a sound commercial venture, the decision to become involved was primarily based on a genuine interest in the Club and a willingness to come forward with financial backing when the opportunity arose. For the same reasons Hayselden has sponsored numerous other local sporting events like the Barnsley Six Road Race and clubs such as Yorkshire County Cricket; it subscribed to the Metrodome, Barnsley's modern sports complex which provides excellent sporting and recreational facilities for the local community, and has also given generous support to many local cricket and football clubs. Outside the sporting sphere, its involvement with the community includes supporting school fetes and many other local clubs and associations. Success has not altered Hayselden's sympathies and loyalties; it is still very much a local firm, sharing the interests and concerns of the community.

Tom Hayselden is now enjoying a well-earned retirement, and his grandson Mark has joined the company. The family sees this continuing commitment, from one generation to the next, as playing a vital part in maintaining the successful formula which has evolved over the years. Similarly, another

Above: *Barnsley playing against Blackburn in October 1981.*
Left: *Barnsley football team in 1981.*

element in this formula is the long-serving workforce. Many of the staff have been at Hayselden for ten or even twenty years, and it is no accident that many key positions in the organisations are occupied by staff who have begun at the bottom of the ladder and worked their way up; Mike Hayselden values his employees and is a keen advocate of keeping a stable workforce. From an insider's point of view, the advantage is that the 'culture' of the company is preserved, with the management policies and working practices remaining consistent and the unsettling effects of unnecessary change being kept to a minimum.

From an outsider's point of view, customers find it reassuring to know that they can come back time after time, and be dealt with, each time, in the same way by the same people. Tom Hayselden believed that one of the most important things was to 'talk to people properly', and the experienced staff at Hayselden have had many years practice at doing just that.

In recent years Hayselden has gone from strength to strength. As well as its two Volkswagen

Top: *Another scene from the match with Shrewsbury.*
Above: *The Barnsley Football Club crest.*

showrooms, it has an Audi centre, a Mazda franchise and a commercial dealership as well as a self-contained paint and bodywork facility. In these days of huge, multi-franchise car groups and the often rather impersonal car supermarkets, it is heartening to see a local, family-owned business can hold its own with the biggest without resorting to the high pressure selling systems adopted by many of its competitors. Managing Director Mike Hayselden is usually to be found on the shop floor at Hayselden's Barnsley branch, chatting to existing customers and new ones, many of whom take him to be just another salesman. It is this ability to stay in touch with the needs of the local people which has charac-terised each generation of Hayseldens, and the motorists of Barnsley have responded by continuing to bring their custom to the dealer whom they know will always give them quality service at a good price.

The reputation which Tom Hayselden began to build up almost forty years ago is stronger than ever today, and the management and staff of Hayselden look forward to living up to that reputation and continuing to serve Barnsley's motorists for the next thirty-nine years and beyond.

Below: The first match of the 1981/82 season, Barnsley v Shrewsbury following promotion to the Second Division.

On the home front

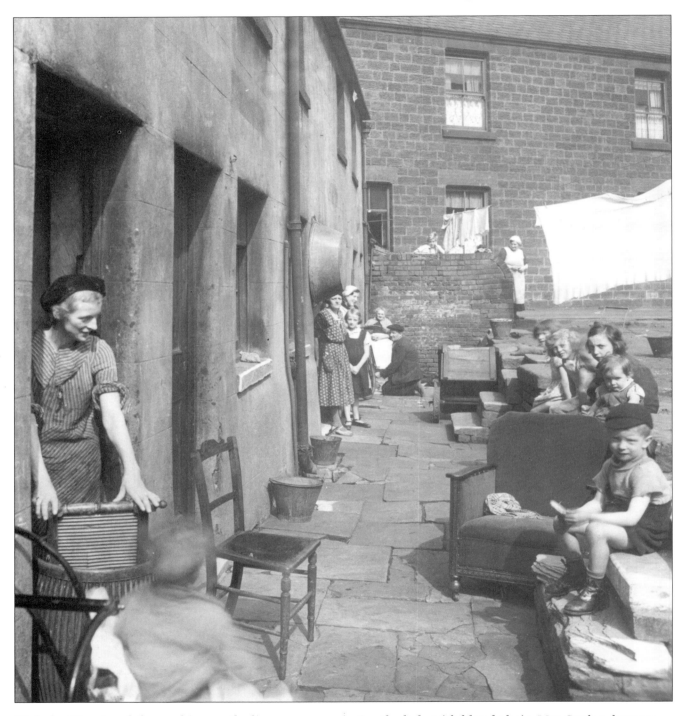

Nicholas Street and the washing on the line are a backdrop to this view of Oak Street off Racecommon Road. We are looking at nos 24, 26, 28, 30 and 32 - a lot of houses in an obvious restricted space in which to live. The bath, the washboard and the tub outside say a lot about the conditions under which these people existed over sixty years ago. The residents of Oak Street may seem contented enough sitting in the sunshine in August 1938 but the need to re-house them is so evident here.

For the lady with blonde hair, Mrs Copley, her two sons, one called Colin, and her daughter, Brenda, for Mrs Allott further up the yard with daughter, Joyce, and for Mrs Naylor, the lady seated in the corner, it will be farewell to one community and, eventually, welcome to another.

The parents will be able to reminisce about these cramped conditions as they give their children the chance to live and play in houses and surroundings they at least deserve.

municipal housing estates in Barnsley, the Lundwood Estate off Pontefract Road with Abbots Road in the process of development. Other estates were established at Wilthorpe, Kendray, Smithies and Ardsley. With the clearance of a lot of old property in the town centre and the building of these estates, the face of Barnsley began to change dramatically.

Top: A look at how we used to live. All the house in one room at number 9 Blucher Street, Court 4 off Wellington Road. This February 1938 photograph had to be taken by flashlight as part of the corporation's application for compulsory purchase of properties in this area of the town in order that they should be demolished. There were many houses in streets such as Wall Street, New Street and Oak Street where it was felt that the conditions under which people lived in terms of sanitation and other issues relating to health mainly, made it important that they should be demolished and the occupants re-housed. So, like all his neighbours, this gentleman will take with him the belongings he has acquired over many years and to which he can relate in terms of experiences and memories in his life and be placed in a house which, for all its amenities, may take some time to call home.

Above: The process of rebuilding Britain after the First World War was a long and slow one. Industry needed to be re-vitalised to bring about the wealth and prosperity to realise a desire to improve the social conditions and living standards of its people. The government had urged councils to build 'homes fit for heroes'. Barnsley responded by following the lead of all other towns and looked for land on its edges to build, as well as sweeping away the cramped and unhealthy town centre slums. Here we see one of the first

Bird's eye view

The Railway Bridge across Eldon Street from the Court House Station gives a lead to our tour of central Barnsley in the 1950s. The market's popularity is at its height here and we can see the extent to which it dominated this part of the town. On the other side of May Day Green is the old Littlewoods store and close by are the Corporation Buildings. Woolworth's original store on Queen Street backs up to Eldon Street and at the top corner where both streets meet is the unique frontage of Burtons. The extent to which the Public Hall dominates the central area is plain to see here as is the majesty of the Regent Street Congregational Church. The Court House to the left of the church still retains its function but the buildings today on the street do not possess the same authority as those when this photograph was taken. Barnsley Building Society and the businesses of Market Hill take us back to Queen Street and the old Yorkshire Bank premises. On the opposite corner is Market Street, looking more imposing here from this height than it does at ground level today.
No Town Hall to dominate this photograph, just the area of the town for which Barnsley was renowned - the Market.

Barnsley in 1958 has a pattern of streets which are easy to define, especially here as the Town Hall makes a good starting point. Behind this 1930s building is the Churchfields site of the police and fire stations. To their left on Westgate is the then very active Barnsley Boys Club. The six roads meeting at Town End allow us a look at the distinctive chimney of Race Street Swimming Baths and the Princess Picture Palace. Further down Peel Street is Freeman's Suba Seal works, the scene of was at one time Barnsley's biggest ever fire. Peel Square does not lose its shape over the years and at the corner of Queen Street and Eldon Street is the white frontage of Burton's tailoring with the floors above given over to the Cuban Dance Hall. The market area around May Day Green dominates the lower left and we pass the fun fair of Barnsley Feast actually in full swing before we head for the bus station, the Queens Hotel and the Court House Station. At the top of Regent Street, appearing to be under the Town Hall, is the site of the old Post Office and below it, set back from the road, is the old billiard hall.

There have been changes since this photograph was taken.

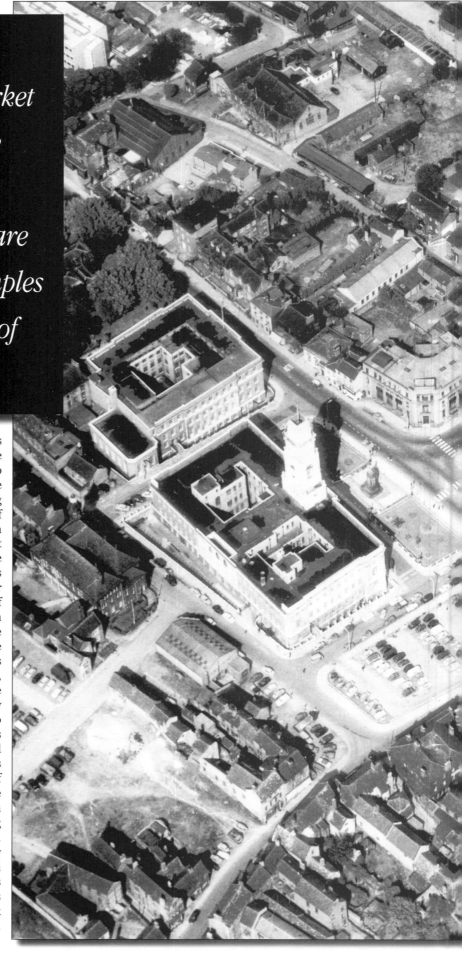

The line of buildings up Market Street, past the junction with Shambles Street are outstanding examples of architecture of the time

Many fine buildings dominate this 1961 photograph in addition to the Town Hall and Technical College. To the left are the Barnsley Chronicle offices and works. Barnsley Building Society Offices stand on the corner of Regent Street and at its corner with Eastgate are the County Court Offices. Further down the street are the premises of then Eyre Brothers Garage which now have another function these days. The lofty spire of Regent Street Congregational Church is very distinct here. The roof of the grand Civic Hall stands out and as we come up the street there is Harralls jewellers and the Three Cranes Hotel, At the corner with Queen Street the white front of what is now McDonalds is plain to see and next to it is the Royal Oak Inn. Woolworths completes that side of the street and back at the bottom of Market Hill is the Yorkshire Bank. The line of buildings up Market Hill, past the junction with Shambles Street and on to Church Street, are outstanding examples of architecture of the time. Included in those would be the now Nat West Bank and the then Butterfield and Massies Drapers opposite the corner with Shambles Street with the original Barclays Bank across the road from the Town Hall.

The lower parts of this 1968 view of Barnsley shortly before re-development alters the face of much of the town centre is taken up with the town's industry. The Electricity and Gas Works round Gas Nook stand on one side of the rail line and over the level crossing on the other are the CEAG premises. May Day Green and the market with the Cross Keys Inn lead us past the Burlington Arcade towards the market stalls on Market Hill and then to Shambles Street. On the other side of the Town Hall is the Technical College. Victoria Road and Huddersfield Road lead to new Technical College buildings. Opposite the Civic Hall is Eldon Arcade and at the end of Eldon Street at the corner of Regent Street is the Queens Hotel but the Court House Railway Station had been taken out of use the previous year. To complete the picture is the white topped, purpose-built bowling alley, with the Baba club at the bottom end.

Events & occasions

Below: The 27th August 1921 was a busy day for the Prime Minister, David Lloyd George, on his visit to the area. There was the pleasant duty of a wedding to attend, that of Sir William Sutherland to Annie Christine Fountain at Darton Parish Church and the more public function of inspecting the soldiers of the York and Lancaster Regiment in Eldon Street. The title of the regiment was derived from the two duchies of York and Lancaster and this was truly a local affair as the men were recruited from the Sheffield, Rotherham and Barnsley areas.

The regiment had fought with honour in the 'war to end all wars' at places like Paschendale, the Somme and Gallopoli so it would be for Lloyd George a chance to pay tribute to them. As Prime Minister during most of the war, it was he who had to guide the country to a victory of sorts and after it to bring about the economic recovery that the country needed. The war had drained not only the country's coffers but almost a whole generation of the country's men.

Right: The crowds line the route, the civic dignitaries parade behind in their limousines and leading the way is the Barnsley British Co-operative Society's band. You can almost hear that drum! The occasion was the celebration of the Silver Jubilee of His Majesty King George 5th's accession to the throne. He had visited Barnsley in 1912, the year of the miners' strike, and that strike had distressed him greatly. But today the country had something to celebrate and like all other towns Barnsley had its own Jubilee procession. London, that evening, was described as 'a city of brilliant light'. A crowd of over 150,000 stood outside Buckingham Palace for the appearance of the King and Queen. When he did appear on the balcony with his grandchildren, Elizabeth and Margaret Rose, in the late evening, he then pressed a button - a bonfire burst into flame and a chain of two thousand beacon fires blazed from hilltops round the country. So in May 1935 Barnsley, like the rest of the country, could celebrate something worthwhile for the first time since the end of the Great War in 1918.

Left: 'Laughter and joy shall be untaxed. No 40 hour week for merrymaking. Long live the Carnival. Coffers are to be opened'. These were the slogans of Worsborough Dale's Miss Mary Goulding, Carnival Queen for Barnsley's 'Joy Week' in 1936 in the town's effort to raise funds for Beckett Hospital and other local charities. The week started off with this street procession and the events during the next seven days included a fun fair, a Punch and Judy show, a Boxing display by the Barnsley Boys Club, a Keep-fit one by the men's section of the Council for Social Service and Dancing displays by the Snow Academy, the Marie Bell and the Avis Tonge Schools and also a concert by the Ward Green Harmonic Society. Other events included a Motor-cycle Gymkhana, a baby show, the pantomime, 'Cinderella', performed by St Barnabas Welfare Society, and ox-roasting. The last Saturday was given over to a physical culture display by Silkestone Boys Club, a cabaret and the Royston WEA Dramatic Group presenting 'The Merchant of Venice'. Let the Carnival Queen have the last word - 'Let joy be unrestrained'.

Above: A tumultuous welcome was given to King George 5th and Queen Mary on their visit to the town on 10th July 1912.
The Mayor, Councillor J H Cotterill, called the visit 'a red letter day for the inhabitants'. The town of Barnsley had prepared itself for the visit of the grandparents of the present Queen with streets, houses, shops, civic buildings and businesses decorated with flags and bunting and many bearing banners proclaiming the town's loyalty.
The weather was described as 'glorious' for the fifty minute stay before the royal couple left for Sheffield, part of the royal tour of South Yorkshire. Thousands of people lined the route of the procession, which included Market Hill, Queen Street, Cheapside, Sheffield Road and Doncaster Road. In fact the calvacade's progress was considerably slowed up by the mass of crowds on Market Hill. A local report at the time remarked on 'the welkin ringing with the acclamation of a delighted populace' and that aptly sums it up.

Below: This is not a street party to celebrate VE Day, the wedding of the Princess Elizabeth or her Coronation in June 1953 but of the marriage of the Queen's sister, Margaret to Mr Anthony Armstrong-Jones in May 1960. The ceremony took place in Westminster Abbey in front of two thousand guests many of whom could watch it on closed-circuit television, the first time this had ever been used in the Abbey, with an estimated television audience of three million people around the world. Crowds, the biggest in London since the Coronation, gathered to watch the processions and later wait while the couple set off on their honeymoon in the Caribbean on the Royal Yacht, Britannia. Like at all joyous national occasions, the mums and the occasional dad set out the tables and chairs in New Street, Great Houghton, cakes and sandwiches were made, there was bound to be jelly and ice-cream and pop and games afterwards and the children, with their lives in front of them, can celebrate the future of the newly married couple.

Right: 'Since the war began, the Government has received countless enquiries from men of all ages who wish to do something for the defence of their country' broadcast a Minister as the German tanks rolled into France at the beginning of the Second World War. As a result there sprung up organisations like the Home Guard, as it was later called, and the ARP, while existing volunteer organisations like the St John's Ambulance Brigade. became a vital part of this defence team. By the end of June 1940 the ARP, made up of women and those men too old for active service, became part of the force which was prepared to defend Britain part-time without pay and as we can see here in Goldthorpe without uniform, the only means of identification being the warden's arm band. Their equipment consisted of a gas-mask, an air-raid warning whistle and a torch. An ARP warden summarised the job as 'no plums, just raspberries'. As the war progressed and the bombing of our cities and industrial towns increased, the work of the ARP and the St John's Ambulance Brigade was so dangerous that by September 1942 more civilians than servicemen had been killed and injured.

Bottom: The girls of the High School parade for the camera in 1946 after a BBC broadcast. The school was founded in 1905 and moved to its new building on Huddersfield Road in 1909. There were over 400 pupils on roll then and, being in a new building, the facilities offered to the girls were extensive. The main features, other than the seventeen classrooms, were a large assembly hall, an Art room and rooms to teach Science. This was at a time when much of Science was considered not to be a 'girl's subject'. More in keeping with contemporary thought were the facilities to learn cookery and laundry work. The school was able to increase its numbers after the Great War and it went from strength to strength acquiring a reputation for providing quality education for girls whose fees in 1936 were £9.9s a year. Its recent history shows that it became part of the local comprehensive system in 1973, a sixth form college in the 1980s and now part of Barnsley Technical College. In the peace time of 1946 these girls would be able to appreciate their education with 'good prospects'.

Right: A 4th form class in 1947 at Barnsley Technical School.

The passage of time has resulted in some of the surnames being forgotten by the person who donated the otherwise delightfully nostalgic picture. Perhaps someone with a better memory than us could fill in the gaps for us for the sake of future reprints of this book? Back: Audrey Kirk, Mary Harrison, Elaine Brook, Edna Walker, Ruth Stevenson, Alice Holling, Jennifer Crossland, Doris Hazeldine, June Richardson. Middle: Ethel Robinson, Betty, Vera Chapman, Rowena, Margaret Fellows, Thelma Hooley, Alisa Jones, Elise Gibson, Gwyneth Harris, Brenda Ainley. Front: Miss Hardy, Doris Page, Pat Jackson, Joan Brown, Betty Crossland, Joan, Sylvia , May Oughton, Connie, Maureen Chappell, Evelyn Simpson. A few memories there and lots to talk about. Where are they now we wonder?

Current television series show that fire brigades are made up of a few firewomen doing the same job as the men and in real life it is standard practice in brigades in this country to have women 'on the strength'. During the horrors of the bombing in the Second World War the job of fighting fires was undertaken by many women but it took a long time before they were allowed to resume that role. In the 1960s in the Barnsley Borough Fire Brigade there were firewomen but their duties were confined to the control room rather than to the actual fire fighting which was still reserved only for the men. The ladies lined up here for their tea break at the new Broadway Fire Station are from left to right, Mary Long, Mary Betts, Joyce Fuller, Kath Reynolds, Julie Beard and Ethel Brisbane.

Above: September 1933 and an engineer inspects the clock in the new Barnsley Town Hall immediately after its installation. The original design of the Town Hall included a spire but that was never built. It had replaced the old town hall in St Mary's Gate, a building not noted for its size or beauty and not befitting a town with the growing status at that time of Barnsley. Many towns and cities in northern England possess some distinctive and wonderful civic buildings and local authorities have tried hard to ensure that their town halls remain as landmarks. Others have not and allowed the near surrounds to almost cloak fine examples of civic architecture. Barnsley is fortunately in the former category and the Town Hall is THE centre of Barnsley. Every town needs a civic focal point and this 1933 building and the impressive area containing the War Memorial are just that.

Below: A photograph of the resplendently dressed Barnsley Accordion Band in 1959 taken at the Old Arcadian Hall, Market Street. Standing are drummers Keith Greasby and Horace Crossland Back row: Phillip Burkinshaw, Joan Milnes, Hazel Taylor, Mavis Simms, Pauline Holmes, Phillip Watson Front row: Barry Crossland, Pearl Fawcett, Bobby Russell, Margaret Collins, Joan Rawlings Stalwarts of the band since the beginning of the decade are Margaret Collins, Barry and Horace Crossland, Phillip Watson, Bobby Russell and the man on the drums, Keith Greasby. The band's reputation was well-earned for it was British Champions on several occasions and band members won solo and duet championships at that level as well. The band disbanded about 10 years ago but had the pleasure not so long ago of a celebratory reunion when drummer Keith Greasby reached a certain birthday.

Barnsley Accordion Band played concerts mostly for charity all over Yorkshire

Barnsley Accordion Band in 1954 at the YMCA, Eldon Street showing their prizes.
Back row: Barry Crossland, Tony Webster, Stan Perkins Middle Row: Elaine Taylor, Dorothy Hewitt, June Wilkinson, Shirley Mudd (vocalist)
Standing: Pearl Fawcett, Margaret Collins, Horace Crossland, Phillip Watson, Bobby Russell.
The Band was formed in the late 1940s following the lead of the Bells Accordion Band. The original rehearsal rooms were at the Wheatsheaf on Racecommon Road, the Lord Nelson on Shambles Street, the chapel on Blucher Street, the YMCA and the local USDAW branch offices. It was a family affair with the Crossland family, father, son and daughter, Hazel, some of the mainstays.
The band played concerts mostly for charity and not only in this area but all over Yorkshire as its fame spread. This was a popular band with real musical talent and if the audiences enjoyed the listening as much as the band enjoyed the playing they would be well satisfied.

Left: This photograph may bring back some memories of schooldays for it is the staff of Barnsley Technical School in 1947. All very formal, no first names or initials and not a nickname to be seen. Back: Miss Morris, Miss Frost, Miss Richardson, Mrs Lister, Miss Hoyden, Miss Burchel, Miss Remmington, Mrs Leach, Mr McMullen. Middle: Mr Seaman, Mr Prendergast, Mr Gibson, Mr Hook, Mr Westwood, Mr Wilson, Mrs Griffiths, Anon, Mr Chambers. Front: Mr Blackburn, Miss Busfield, Mrs Jones, Mr Williamson, Mr Chadwick, Mr Pilkington, Miss Lawton, Mr Hill, One member of staff whose name is missing. Any offers?

Below: A photograph to be treasured of the happy smiling class of Mr Goddard in the sunshine at Keir Street School in the 1950s. Unfortunately the children seated on the ground at the front have not been identified for us. It also appears that there were two girls with the same name in the class with a 'royal' way of identifying them. Bet they caused poor Mr Goddard some headaches if that were the case. To bring back some memories of the happiest days of their lives we have:- Back: Pat Johnson, Rosemary Peake, Anne Bradley, Carol Goddard, Angela Bradley, Hazel Crossland (1st) Middle: Ralph Kay, Elaine Braithwaite, Alan Clay, Wendy Roberts, Lorraine Ward, Ian Earnshaw, Kathleen Bennett, Ron Laughton Front: Jean Hanson, David Rose, Sandra Jenkinson, Frankie Killburn, Mr Goddard, Roger Coldwell, Hazel Crossland (2nd), Jimmy Thornton On ground - unidentified but not for long hopefully.

Above: Police Motor cycles bearing the Barnsley HE registration are all lined up with their riders equally as smart for their turn in the Annual Inspection of the Borough Police by Home Office Inspector of Constabulary, Mr Brownlow. Shades of 'The Bill'. With him looking somewhat anxious is the Borough's Chief Constable, Mr G Parfitt, and on the right is Scotsman PC Eddy Gilmartin. Inspections were the occasions for a 'bit of bull'. Everything inside and outside the station was made spick and span - the cells, interview room, control room, the workshops. The books were inspected, the bosses interviewed and many a young PC was dropped on with an awkward question which he and his sergeant hoped he got right, especially as he would be rather nervous anyway on parade. None more so than one young copper who left his Brylcreem sticking out of his tunic pocket when he lined up for inspection and Inspectors don't miss much.

Above right: In the days when inspections aroused a great deal of trepidation in the members of the Fire Brigade and the Inspector himself was a man from the Home Office whose name you were probably never told and even if you were told, it was not so important to remember it, then it is no wonder there is scarcely a smile on the faces of the firewomen of the Barnsley

Borough Fire Brigade. They try to appear to be relaxed as they are lined up but can recall the rigours of the days prior to the inspection when they had to remember more important things than the name of the Inspector.Accompanying him on this 1962 inspection is the Borough's Chief Constable, Mr Parfitt, the Mayor, Councillor H Dancer, and the chairman of the Watch Committee, Mr J Wood. Looking on, hoping his charges put on a good show, is ADO Wardman and undergoing the questioning is Firewoman Cynthia Woodhouse.

The chance to show off your knowledge to the Home Office Inspector as the men of the Barnsley Borough Fire Brigade wait for the awkward question from the Home Office Inspector in 1962.
The Chief Fire Officer, F R Hall, appears to have complete confidence in Firemen Harry Tyler, Don Ball, Albert Lawrence and Joe Johnson to deliver the goods and councillors waiting in the rear and spectators looking out of windows would be anxious that the good name of the brigade is maintained.

These were the days when towns like Barnsley had their own borough fire brigade and police force and it was not until the re-organisation of local government in the 1970s that the control past to newly created county authorities.
Whether that pride of belonging to the town's brigade was ever the same under a larger organisation at county level is difficult to say, but if it made the service even more efficient then the public would be satisfied.

Left: Clutching his school cap, young Brian Holden is presented to her Majesty in front of civic dignitaries including the long serving town clerk, Mr A E Gilfillan, and guests representing the Co-operative movement, the National Union of Mineworkers, the Mining Industry, the Glass Industry and other local businessmen. As a memento of her visit the Queen was given a model pit tub bearing the Royal coat of arms, the arms of the Borough and the crest of the National Coal Board. This piece of unique crafts-manship was made by students from the Technical College. The Prince was given a model miner's electric lamp made by CEAG Ltd. Once the ceremonials were over, the royal couple drove through the town, thrilling the large crowds, including over 12,000 children strategically positioned along the route. In the days when royal lives were not under such public scrutiny, this was a day to remember for Barnsley and public celebrations lasted long after the couple had crossed the borough boundary.

Above: Following in the footsteps of her father, George 6th and her grandfather George 5th, the newly crowned Queen, Elizabeth 2nd and Prince Phillip visited the town in October 1954 and the reception given to her by the people of Barnsley was described as 'rousing'. Here in front of the distinguished array of guests representing all facets of local civic and business life is schoolgirl Pauline Brooker being introduced to Her Majesty by the Mayor, Alderman Alfred Edward McVie CB JP. Waiting his turn to meet her on behalf of all schoolchildren of the borough like Pauline is Brian Holden. Six hundred other Barnsley schoolchildren formed a choir to sing two songs in honour of the guests, appropriately 'English Rose' and 'In Loyal Bond United', while the Regimental Band of the York and Lancaster Regiment provided other music. In fact the band never seemed to stop playing all day for they performed in the afternoon and gave a concert in the evening on this momentous day for the town.

Bottom: A combined Christmas and New Year drink in January 1967 from Grenville Moore, the manager of the Alhambra Odeon Cinema, to his staff from left to right, Helen Froggatt, Eileen Wilmott, Ada Bulmer, Alice Hayward, Louie Birkin, Clare Hatton and Doreen Hough.
It is doubtful whether these ladies and Mr Moore could cast their minds back to when the Alhambra became part of the Gaumont cinema circuit in 1926. It remained part of that age when cinema going was THE form of entertainment through the 1930s, even through the war years until the decline in the 1960s when television and other forms of entertainment overtook the cinema. When the new Gaumont was opened in Eldon Street in 1956, the cinema changed its name to the Odeon. The very last film at the Odeon on 26th November 1960 was 'The Entertainer', starring Laurence Olivier and had that famous Scott Joplin rag to provide appropriate background music. So after thirty four years of providing cinema entertainment the Alhambra Odeon finally succumbed to the lure of Bingo.

Below right: Two old stagers sit and reminisce about the old times as officers in the Barnsley Borough Police at gathering of old force members for the twenty-fifth anniversary of the ending of close knit county borough police forces at the beginning of the 1970s. The controlling authority was at county level now, as with the fire brigade. The idea of identifying with the

Borough police was strong with the men and there would be a lot to talk about at this reunion of the members of the force. It would be a great opportunity for ex-PCs Bill Harber and John Todd to remind each other of colleagues, of felons and drunks, of sergeants and inspectors and chief constables, incidents and arrests, parades, processions and celebrations, point duty at busy junctions, like on Cheapside, and all the other matters that made their policeman's lot 'such a happy one' - well if not blissful, then memorable.

A few not so dry eyes here in this line up of staff of the Alhambra Odeon in 1960 at the farewell presentation to Mary Senior who was about to emigrate to Australia. All the staff are present here which says a lot for the guest of honour and for the spirit of co-operation among the members. Men in the back row from left to right : Mr D Pritty, Mr Bailey, Jim Greenhough, Brian Cooper, Harry Renshaw, Granville Moore (Manager) and to his right the doorman, Bill Heath. Ladies at the back between Renshaw and Moore: Joyce Wood, Frances Allan nee Wood, Margaret Youell. Ladies standing: Eileen Wilmott, Mary Stott, Alice Haywood, Louie Birkin, Doris Rowell, the guest of honour, then Lucy Lockwood-Dukes, Lily Firth.
Kneeling: Iris Hunter, Ada Bulmer, Kathy Tales. The photographer was Stan Bulmer.

Above: A blast from the past and a chance to ask 'Where are they now?' as the high-powered Barnsley Licensed Victuallers Association assemble with their guests for their annual dinner in the early 1960s. The team sheet reads:- Back: J Crossley, Woodmoor, Carlton; E Rose, Elm Tree, Worsborough Dale; T Walsh, Fitzwilliam, Barnsley; J McNally, St George, Wombwell; H Ryder, Rose and Crown, Mt Vernon; A Price, Acourt, Athersley; A Turner, King George, Barnsley; D Bailey, Railway, Royston; E Clowey, Sportsman, Smithies; W Boyland, Periwinkle, Wombwell; F Bailey, Barley Sheaf, Wombwell; E Plews, Coach and Horses, Ardsley. Front: S Addy, Butchers Arms, Monk Bretton; Chief Superintendent Dearden, Barnsley Borough Police; a Brewery Rep.; G Armitage, Wellington, Athersley; E Stainrod (President), Masons Arms, Worsborough Dale; A Hirst (Junior Vice Pres.), Rose and Crown, Penistone; M Hepworth (Secretary), Horse and Jockey, Dodworth; T Jones (John Smith's Brewery); M Williamson (Mansfield Brewery). Pubs had 'proper' names in those days!

Right: Down with the old and in with the new in December 1969 as the planners and developers tear out the heart of Cheapside at its meeting with New Street, Pontefract Road and Sheffield Road. There is a little interest in the crane and the bulldozer as some memories are stirred as to the exact location of the old Woolworths building, Evans, Principals and Paiges near the surviving Burlington Arcade. It is often

hard to visualise a shop, seemingly so large when standing, appearing to have been so small in area when reduced to rubble. But time forces change as commerce and property development march on. The old Victorian townscapes are replaced by other, larger and more functional but often less elegant. Shops multiply and the demand for a wider range of goods has to be met. The national chains like Woolworths, WH Smiths, Marks and Spencer, Boots and Burtons, with its associated shops, largely begin to take over the high street and many local ones either re-locate or close down

Inset: The Corporation Buildings on Pontefract Road looking towards May day Green and housing the offices of the Barnsley Executive Council of the National Health Service with its downstairs neighbour in Curtess Shoes feel the judder and the power of demolition. It is December 1969 and Barnsley is undergoing a structural change which will seem to go on for ever. From all this the town is promised shopping centres with bright attractive hallways which will be easy to find your way around. There will be a more than ample number of attractive cafes to take the weight off your feet and relax in. There will be well known department and specialist shops and everything you want will be in walking distance in the safe and pleasant environment of a pedestrianised centre. There will be ample parking on the doorstep. What more could you ask for?

Below: Crossing the bridge to the market the royal couple made it a point to talk to members of the guard of honour formed from representatives of the Guides, the Scouts, the Army and Sea Cadets and members of the Fire Service. The walkabout in the festooned market complex gave the Prince a chance to order a black pudding which was eventually delivered to him in Sheffield later in the visit ready for his return to London. The Queen stopped for a chat with the teachers and pupils from eleven local schools who were given a special place in the Hall. The visit was a special thrill for royal fanatic, Kathleen Roffey of Athersley Street, who had stapled all manner of Union Jacks to her trousers and hat. Whether the royal couple noticed her is not on record but many others did and Kathleen was quite a fashion 'hit' for the day. The visit ended all too soon with a walk down Cheapside to the royal car and a short drive to the station for the just as short train journey to Sheffield. Once again Barnsley had given special honour to its sovereign. ·

Right: The headline stated 'Barnsley rolls out the carpet for the royal couple' and the less formal aspects of current royal visits were demonstrated in Her Majesty the Queen's visit with Prince Phillip to Barnsley in July 1975. Twenty thousand people had gathered in sweltering heat to see their Majesties, their first visit here for twenty-one years. The ceremonial was still evident as the pair were greeted by the Mayor, Councillor Harold Brain, civic officials and County Council Officers at the new County Offices. Music was provided by the Grimethorpe Colliery Band and bouquets presented by Gillian Brain and Anne Burkenshaw. The more informal aspects of their fifty-five minute stay in the town occured with the walk from the new County Offices to the equally as new Market complex when they met members of the vast crowd including several senior citizens and four lucky schoolboys from Royston, Paul Todd, Peter Green, Wayne Derby and Geoffrey Miller.

On the move

Cheapside contained some of the more celebrated shopping names in Barnsley

Above: Traffic is making very slow headway on the part of Sheffield Road where it drops down from below Park Road into Cheapside. The re-surfacing work collects its fair share of interested certainly and critical possibly spectators and shoppers' progress is being impeded by it all. The road contained some of the more celebrated shopping names in Barnsley like Horsfields at nos 59 to 63 on the right below the Odeon. This shop like the others closed in 1971. Its windows were a mini department store of its own as it could in one cramped space display all manner of boots and shoes, quilts, watches and suits among other things as well as being, like Harrals on the same road, a pawnbroker. There was the grocery department of the co-op here, Cantor's furniture store across the road from the Odeon, which closed in 1969, Palmer's drapers shop and next door at 154 its grocers shop. Like the market you could buy anything on this street from sewing machines to toys to motor cycles; no wonder Bovril was advertised so prominently, a shopper would need it after a trip here to all those shops.

Below: A very smartly dressed foreman oversees the work on Sheffield Road outside the Ebenezer Methodist Chapel at the Doncaster Road fork. The chapel, opened in 1873, was a popular place of worship until its closure on Easter Sunday 1975. With the amount of terraced housing in streets and roads branching off, the need for churches like this and St Johns and St Peters together with other smaller chapels was apparent. At right angles to the rest of the buildings is the Manx Arms, known previously as the Legs of Man and the Baltic Inn and a more appropriate name for the county, The Cricketers Arms. The list of public houses is a long one and includes the Alhambra Hotel, the Spotted Leopard and opposite the Rising Sun. There was also the Victoria Hotel which closed in 1973 and the Clarence Hotel was once the headquarters of Barnsley AFC. One wag was made to comment that Horsfields and Harralls knew what they were doing when they set up here with so many pubs in the vicinity.

Left: A 1954 view of a part of the town that is just a memory now as Sheffield Road, below its junction with Wesley Street, is in the process of being re-surfaced. The Alhambra Odeon, a cinema still at this time and situated where the road meets with Doncaster Road, has an imposing presence almost out of keeping with the rest of the buildings in the area.

Another cinema in this part of the town on Britannia Street was the Star which stopped showing films about this time. The more popular name for it was 'The Big Hut' and, like other cinemas in the town, Saturday matinees were a weekend treat for noisy children and often a nightmare for the manager and his staff. The area continued to attract shops and shoppers until the plans to re-develop it and it is still hard to imagine that all this is now part of the Alhambra Centre and the Westway road, the shops the pubs and houses having been devoured by it all.

Crowds gather in Barnsley station to photograph, or just stare at, or recall memories of a nearly forgotten sight on the railway lines of the country. The decision in 1968 by British Railways to do away with steam could have meant that the sight of a steam locomotive hauling a train was gone for ever. The efforts of steam enthusiasts paid off. The eight-day exhibition tour by the 'King George V' in 1971 was a resounding success with thousands of people flocking to see the train. As a direct consequence twelve steam-hauled trains were sanctioned to run on main lines in 1972. The return in 1973 of LNER'S the 'Flying Scotsman' from America set the seal of success on all this hard work and it became part of the band of 'limited editions' of locomotive preserved to haul excursions and undertake promotional tours round the country. One enthusiast described it thus 'There is nothing to match the awesome power of an express locomotive hauling a heavy train at main line speeds'. Look at crowds who flock to the private steam lines preserved around the country or to the railway museums for evidence of that enthusiasm.

the story of coal, the coalminers and others who played a part in the life and times of this industry.

Top: A class five steam locomotive 4-6-0 number 44971 leaving Cudworth in September 1967 on the run from Sheffield to Leeds. There were eight hundred and forty-two Class five locomotive built for the old LMS and were popularly known as 'Black Fives'. The magic of steam to many people is indefinable and to them the steam locomotive is almost a living thing. It is not just collecting engine numbers, a hobby many a young lad would do before he developed other interests, but something one steam fan calls 'an incurable disease'. When the curtain was finally rung down on steam on British Railways in August 1968, shortly after this photograph was taken, it was decreed that no preserved steam locomotive would be allowed to run on British Rail lines. The powers of British Rail, however, did not reckon with the enthusiasm and determination of Steam Preservation Societies and three years later one steam locomotive undertook a eight day exhibition tour and thousands of people flocked to see it. Thus began a movement which has not stopped growing.

Above: The rear of Cliffe Bridge Methodist Chapel in the Rotherham Road area of Barnsley overlooks the Oaks Viaduct and adjacent was the Barnsley Main Colliery. The 'Push and Pull' from Cudworth Station to Barnsley Court House ran across the viaduct on the Hull and Barnsley Line. The viaduct was demolished in 1968 and the whole area, once so much a part of Barnsley's industrial life, is now a part of the Dearne Valley Walk and Country Park. The reminders of the mining past of Barnsley gond that of the rest of this part of Yorkshire, are found on the Yorkshire Mining Heritage Trail, a living museum of the places and people integral to

The return fare to Manchester by train was 4/6 when this photograph was taken! The railway station is to the left of the picture but the pride of place must go to the bus station opened in 1938. The central island building housed the 3d bit magazine kiosk, a cafe to seat one hundred and toilets with hot running water. The staff had its own canteen and rest room and there were four platforms linked by a crossing zone. Here the Sheffield bus has just arrived and is waiting to park beyond the staff area as long as that bus in front gets a move on.

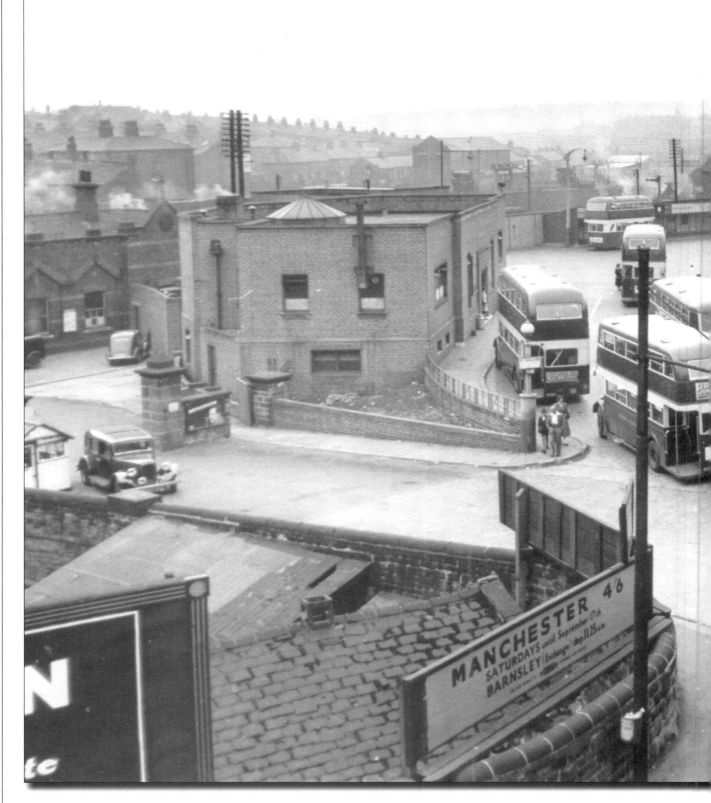

The bus to Bradford is causing a hold up it seems, although someone is surely not using the official safety crossings. All is peaceful at the stands for Darfield Road, Monk Bretton and Lundwood although those three men who are talking together are a suggestion of a queue for the Darfield Road bus. An efficient public transport system was a matter of civic pride to a town when owning a car was a luxury and Barnsley considered its bus station and the service it provided to be 'the best in Yorkshire'.

Below: The 148 Barnsley Squadron of the Air Cadet Force held its 1954 annual camp at RAF Binbrook The magnificent aircraft behind the group is the English Electric Canberra B2 of RAF 617 Squadron. The front row of the group contains the following:-
Flight Sergeant RB Rogers; Flight Lieutenant CBA Brown MBE; Cadet F Wright: Flying Officer DR Broadhead and finally Sergeant G Sowerby.
These annual camps allowed the members of the force to experience at first hand life in the Royal Air Force and also gave a sense of realism to the theory. The aircraft here was in 1954 the most sophisticated the RAF possessed. The thrill of visiting such establishments would have whetted the appetite of many a young man and the thought of a career in the RAF would then seem a glorious prospect.

Right: At the annual camps of the Air Cadet Force the cadets were sometimes given the chance to experience a flight in an aircraft. This time at RAF Scampton the members and officers were given the opportunity of a flight in this Kirby Cadet Mk 3 glider. Because there were so many of the force attending and time allocated was short, the flight comprised a winched take-off, a brief but exciting tour over the airfield and a bumpy landing. To the cadets that may not have been enough, maybe, especially when there is all that sky and countryside to view but 'orders is orders' and that would be better than nothing. Here with the instructor and a cadet in the glider, we see guest photographer, Stan Bulmer, waiting his turn - a flight being a perk of the trade, perhaps. He did decline the offer of going solo!

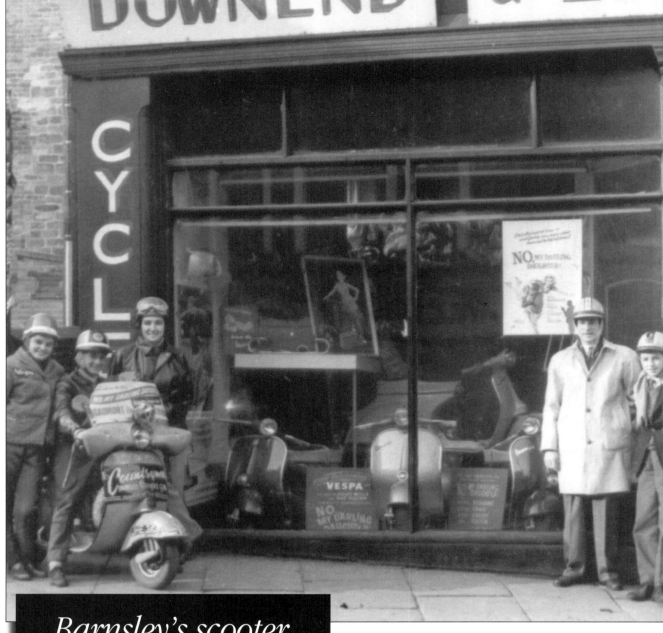

Barnsley's scooter club paraded around the town to attract custom for the Gaumont Cinema in Eldon Street

Downend and Lister's cycle shop was situated on Shambles Street on the Rich Lane corner next to the Old Windmill Hotel.

On parade here are not the 'mods' of the day on their Vespas and Lambrettas seeking a confrontation with the local 'rockers' but members of a local scooter club lined up ready with the support of the staff of the shop to help to promote a film at the Gaumont Cinema in Eldon Street during the early 1960s.

Their subsequent tour of the town on their cycles advertising the coming attraction would have raised a few eyebrows but publicity of any kind is better than none in this case.

If the stunt attracted more custom to the cinema and the scooter riders enjoyed the experience, that is all that matters, especially as they would have been given free seats to see the film.

All we need to know is 'What was the film?' It was 'No, My Darling Daughter'. Do you remember the words to the song?

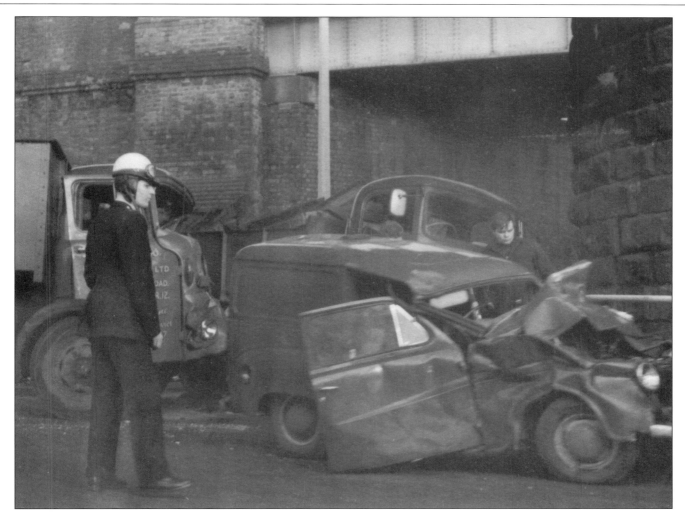

Above: The railway bridge at the Stairfoot cross-roads where the roads to Ardsley and Doncaster meet was notorious in the 1960s for a series of vehicle accidents. Here 2 lorries and a van have met each other head on resulting in what can only be called a pile up. Fortunately no-one was seriously injured in this one but the lorries are a bit of a mess as one seems to have met the wall with some force and the van is an even bigger one. On hand to sort it all out are members of the Borough Police Force with PC John Cooke the officer in attendance and the white helmeted motor cycle policeman PC Sid Oxley ensuring the smooth passage of other vehicles. The area around this infamous junction has now been re-developed with a roundabout to ensure, hopefully, that there are no more serious incidents like this one.

Right: Yorkshire Traction possessed three high speed luxury Leyland coaches for the London 'run' and one of those was allocated to take the Barnsley Football team on to its away fixtures. No wonder Joe Thorpe, the driver, looks proud - luxury coach and local heroes. He had joined the firm in 1919 and retired in 1965 after more than forty-five years of service. The days of Third Division North meant long tours of northern England and the endless road through the Lakes to Workington with no motor way, no service stations and often necessitating an overnight stop. There would not be the amount of travelling away support that occurs today unless there was a derby match so that coach containing among others the team and officials and maybe a pressman may have been the only representatives of the town to those far flung regions. The fortunes of the team in the 1950s and 60s fluctuated and the highs unfortunately were often matched by a period of lows. The worst time must have been the 1952/3 season of relegation from the old Second Division, losing twenty-nine games and winning just five and the high would be under Tim Ward's managership of promotion within the next two years.

DHE 561

Shopping spree

> *These were the days before refrigerators, deep freezers and clingfilm but food stayed fresh wrapped in its cloth*

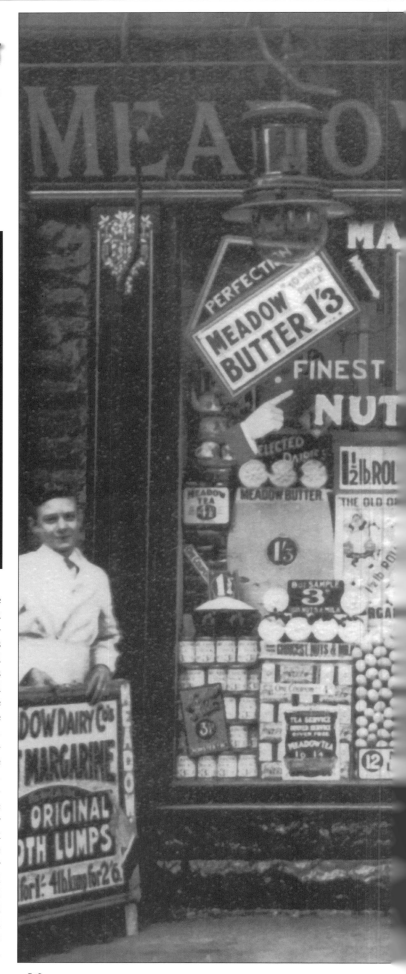

The old post office in Goldthorpe is now the Meadow Dairy in this 1910 photograph. What a turn-out! The four members of staff are immaculately attired and the shop window is just as immaculately dressed. Think of the care and patience to set out that display of the dairy's wares. How did they manage to be so careful and precise with those eggs, the rows of tins, the margarine, the butter, the nuts and those posters? No wonder these men look so proud. They certainly knew about the power of advertising and the attraction of offers when we always thought it was a modern phenomenon. These were the days before refrigerators, deep-freezers and cling film and still the margarine was able to be kept fresh wrapped in cloth rather like the way fresh yeast was served. Did the milk come in churns and be poured out into the customer's own jug? Were there on the counter those metal weighing scales with the ounce and pound weights glistening beside them? May well be, but one thing we can be sure of there would be personal service from these young men. And what became of the Meadow Dairy? It became Rossi's Ice-cream parlour.

Below: 'Barnsley for Bargains' is a good title for this photograph if you think of the teeming market which used to operate three times a week, selling anything a shopper could need. Behind is the Wire Trellis Hotel, certain to revive memories of a long standing landlord, Fred Moxon, and of the crowds who used to regularly frequent it before it finally succumbed to the developers in 1968. So look at the pictures of the old market. Only memories. The new one is on its way. There will have been apprehension about what was to replace it. It will be more comfortable and warmer in Winter, easier to walk around but will it have the same atmosphere? You somehow know, however, that at some point in some future year that when the new has become old and outlived its usefulness and the new market and the new shopping centres surrender to the bulldozer, they too will have a nostalgia of their own.

Right: This photograph of shops on New Street must have been taken before the deliberate spread of myxomatosis in the country which was part of a national cull of the teeming rabbit population. King's fish merchants remained in the street until 1960, having been there since 1898. Schofield's confectionery shop, opened in 1933, left at the same time and both were joined to form Phillip's furnishing store. Meanwhile Brighter Homes remained until 1969. The street's most famous inhabitant was probably the Globe Picture House. The Globe had been opened in 1914 specifically for the showing of silent films and remained a popular place of screen entertainment until the 1960s when it was given over to Bingo. In 1981 it re-opened as the Globe Theatre, hosting amateur and professional productions and there it remained for some years as a tribute to the foresight and hard work of its refurbishers.

Right: Cheapside's most famous inhabitant, Albert Hirst, actually began his butcher's life in Hayes Croft, between Albert Street and New Street. He moved to Cheapside at the turn of the last century and it was here the fame of the Barnsley chop and the Hirst black pudding was forged. The business was carried on by Albert's three sons after he died and Albert, the son, won the European Black Pudding Contest in France and from then on was regarded as the Crowned Black Pudding King. The famous Barnsley Chop was prepared at the Royal Hotel for the Prince of Wales after he had opened the new Barnsley Town Hall in December 1933. With his chop the prince was served chips, followed by tea and toast, peach melba, cheese and biscuits. Whether the Prince, well known for his social life in America, had anything to do with the chop being on the menu at New York's Waldorf Astoria Hotel is a matter of conjecture. Perhaps it is more likely the Hirst reputation did not need royal assistance.

The building, the clock, the chimney, the flagpole - the Barnsley British Co-operative Society Limited. Following the 1844 lead of George Adcroft and the other Rochdale Pioneers, Barnsley's 'Nine Men of Vision' with assets of 9/- in 1861 set out to follow their lead. Their first meeting took place in Tinker's Temperance Hotel in May Day Green and the basis of their philosophy came from the famous Rochdale Principles which included open membership to the society, democratic control and political and religious neutrality, easy to espouse, hard to attain in any era. From this first meeting came the original conditions of membership, the prime one being each member would pay a small sum each week. At the end of the first month the sum of £3.5/- had been collected and the society could boast sixth-eight members at the end of the first year. Within four years and armed with £30, George Kay and his colleagues purchased a small shop on Market Street and so opened the first branch of the Barnsley British Co-op.

When this photograph of Market Hill was taken in 1971, the H-registered Jaguar driving up past the market was almost new. Behind the market stalls we can see Curry's shop sign, but the building next door is for sale through A E Wilby and Son, whose estate agent board was a familiar sight in Barnsley. At the top of the hill, beyond the Town Hall is the imposing Mining and Technical College. Hailed as 'the largest mining college in the country', this College opened in October 1932, at a time when mining was at the heart of Barnsley's economy.

Besides mining, the College offered training in disciplines such as building, electrical engineering, technical drawing, commerce and sciences.
At the bottom of the hill pedestrian guard rails were considered necessary to stop crowds of shoppers spilling off the pavements and onto the road at this junction; as we can see on the right, the rails came in handy for leaning against when waiting for somebody or stopping for a chat. The ornate building on the right had been the Yorkshire Bank since 1903.

A mixture of the old and new in Barnsley in the early 1970s. The old is represented by the chimney of the linen mill, 'Island Corner' at the top of New Street, containing the main premises of the Barnsley Co-op, and the Globe Picture House opened in 1914, converted to bingo in the 1960s revived as a theatre in 1983 and later sadly demolished.

Also there are the shops like Peter Pells and Hardys on Cheapside and finally the last days of the old outdoor market which here cuts a sad sight compared to the life and vitality of the market for which the town was famous.

The new is the modern Market Hall and what is to come here, the Alhambra Centre, named after the old Alhambra cinema which once stood on this site. The new centre will contain shops and cafes in wide walk ways and be close to all the facilities a shopper will need.

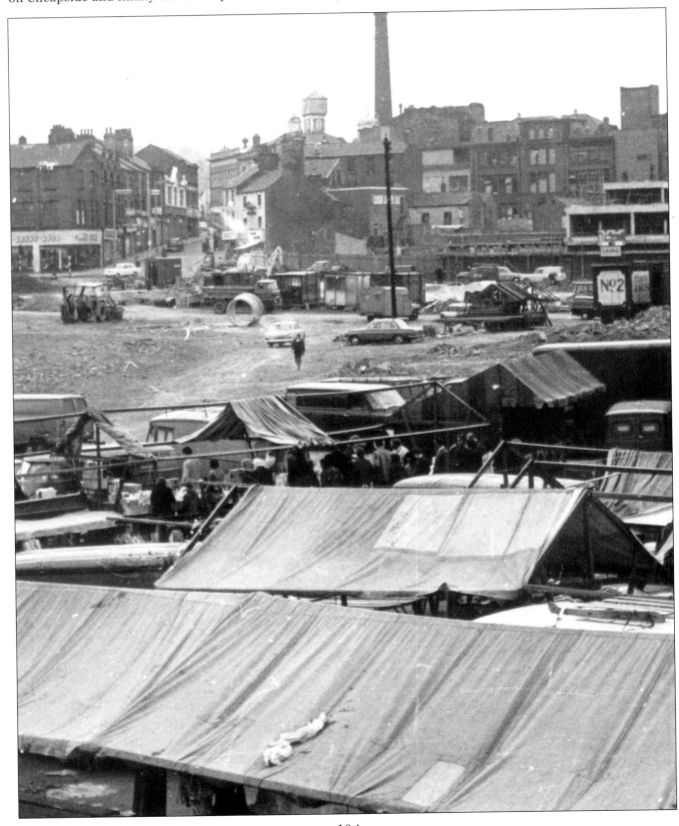

Golden years of **BARNSLEY**

Below: The rear of the Civic Hall, opened in 1878 and presented to the town twelve years later, overlooks the outdoor market in the area of Midland Street and the site of the traditional annual Barnsley Feast. To the left of the Civic Hall is the white frontage of Harrolls Ring Shop, now in the hands of another jeweller. In the market itself are the shops synonymous with this part of the town.

There is Bailey's Chocolate Box and Cafe, Rosenby's bedding and linen shop, Winn's Shoebox and Banks's fish stall. The empty stalls and the equally as empty old cigarette kiosk give the market a sombre appearance but to recall the noise, the hustle and the crowds on Market days would bring back memories of the largest open air market in England where 'if you want we can sell it to you'. The market, given its charter in 1249, is soon to change at this time, however, and its history is to take another turning.

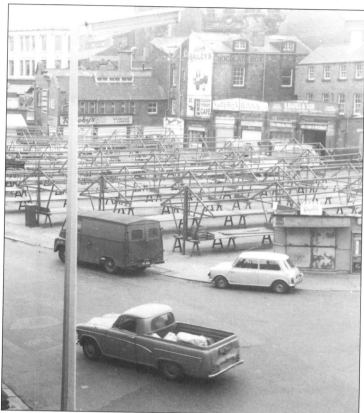

Bottom: A sight of Cheapside from Primrose Hill as the old property is being cleared to give way to the new. The unmistakable curved frontage of the Duke of York Hotel had stood on this site since the 1820s. Farmer's butchers shop was slightly younger as it had only been there since 1901. The struggle of family owned shops to compete in the high street with national chains intensified in the 1960s and it was the W H Smiths, the Burtons, the Boots and other bigger stores who could afford to compete and win, especially as the town centres were in the hands of planners and developers. There was a need to change and to develop if only to cope with the problems caused by traffic. Barnsley's re-development came later than some other northern towns and like them the old town centre landscape was to be swept away and replaced by another, larger and more functional, but possibly less elegant. The number of shops multiplied selling a greater range of goods as there was a growing public demand for more and for the different and Barnsley had to cope with that if nothing else.

The Drug branch of the Co-operative Society on Cheapside is a real 'reminder' to look along the shelves and counter and think 'I used to have Horlicks at night' or 'Do they still make Fynnon Salts?' But really chemist's shops have not changed much except in name of course and nor have their wares and services they provide. There was a pharmacy, a wines and spirits department, opportunity to purchase photographic goods, including a dark room for the demonstration of projectors. It sold the usual surgical goods and there were private rooms for the fitting of elastic trusses and stockings. The co-op could announce that a Max Factor beauty consultant would always be available in the Cosmetics section to give advice and demonstrations on all aspects of beauty culture. An Optician service was also available and really the co-op in this respect was setting the trend for future practices by other such shops. This is one more example of the co-op's influence in the town. It had moved into every area of its members' lives from shops such as this to tailoring, to decorating, to travel and many others; it offered a funeral service and more besides. And it looked after its staff very well indeed.

Left: A hive of equipment from some of the more famous names in the history of radio or to give the proper title Wireless Receiving Station - Mullard. GEC, Marconiphone, Ever Ready - in the radio shop of the Barnsley Co-op when the world was brought to everyone's home as if by magic. This innovative venture was opened in 1920 and was part of the rapid growth of the co-operative movement since those pioneering days in the 1860s. Branch shops had been opened in Dodworth in 1863 and in Wombwell in 1866. By 1962 when the co-op was at its peak, there were 43 branches and 20 mobile shops. A library was established not long after the movement began, a flour mill produced 'Lilywhite' plain flour, a butcher's shop in Market Street was soon opened followed by various others. There was the threepenny stamp club, a savings bank and a welfare fund for members of 40, 50 or 60 years of membership. This radio shop was just one way of the co-op trying to provide everything any member needed, including lessons in Morse Code!

Below: This photograph of the period before the re-development of the town centre is almost a roll call of Barnsley's past as we look at the signs and advertisements in what was the area round Burlington Arcade. The major sign is for Hartle's Good Food market stall proclaiming its dairy products, although whether it actually gave out Green Shield Stamps with each sale is a question unanswered. Zuckers was a long established and well-respected local company famous for its clothing and household textiles. The half-exposed sign belongs to Joe Edwards and his 'pot stall' whose fame spread beyond the borough boundaries. Behind this sign is the end of Wilson's dress shop now the premises of a national chemist store. The near side of the road is now developed and includes a travel agents and a television rental shop while the advertising hoardings tell another story of the times.

Bottom: It is Christmas time at the YEB showroom in Eldon Street and like every other shop in the town in 1949 there is a chance to display seasonal gifts very useful in the home. The authority to supply power to homes, business and industry passed to the state as a result of the post-war Labour government's nationalisation legislation and so regional boards like Yorkshire Electricity were established. The premises were situated underneath the Three Cranes Hotel, the main part of which was in Queen Street. To the left of the Electricity premises was the rear entrance to the hotel; to the right was the other entrance to the hotel and further on was B and C's Manshop. Next to that was the Burlington Arcade and then the Gas Board's Showroom with its neighbour, the original Woolworths, over the Royal Oak Yard. Woolworths extended its store in 1972, six years after the Electricity and Gas boards had vacated their premises.

At work

Below 'We stock everything but the baby' and the famous neon lit iron work sign including the stork can only mean one shop in Barnsley - Bailey's.
Unfortunately the sign underneath tells another story - 'To Let' - as the store in 1968 is about to close after over 80 years here after serving generations of parents and future mams and dads will now have to look elsewhere. The Barnsley British Co-operative store to its left and sharing
the same frontage is to share the same fate and so will the original co-op building, housing the butchery department on the other side as that becomes a branch of Boots.
Littlewoods will move to a new store on the other side of Cheapside and that market area, part of the largest open-air market in England, will be re-developed to make way for it and for other shops as this part of the town is transformed into what is considered to be more appropriate for the changing times.

Right: Peel Street in the 1950s seemed to gather about itself many visiting attractions, possibly because it was the main road to the town centre from the six-junctioned Town End. This gentleman, Mr Strong on his horse and cart selling brushes and pots and pans, was not an attraction but was a regular visitor. Those who did come to earn their bread by entertaining the people who lived and worked and shopped in the street were an organ grinder with his chimpanzee and a trainer with his performing bear. Not necessarily wholesome sights these days but novelties one or two decades ago!
The street was part of the traditional route of the Miners' demonstrations and their banners and bands would be a more welcome sight than a bear or a monkey. But the cream of Peel Street entertainment was the Ritz cinema opened in 1937 with its Art Deco front certainly enhancing the street among the other less decorous buildings.

Barnsley Oakwell Brewery closed its doors in 1973 after brewing beer for eighty-five years

A 1926 view of the new Beevor Hill Bridge over the canal on Pontefract Road as the old bridge is being filled in. Three differing types of industry, famous in the time, stood on either side of the canal itself a vital part commercial life then.

The view we have here is taken from near Woods Glassworks and Wilson and Company's Bobbin Works, the latter closing in 1954. The story of the growth of the glass industry and of the bobbin industry at the beginning of the century is a fascinating account of the use of local resources and labour. The third, and probably most distinguished of the three, can be seen here. It is the Barnsley Oakwell Brewery, including its distinctive malthouses. The brewery closed in February 1973, though not without a long struggle, after brewing beer for eighty-five years.

At one time it owned ninety-three licensed premises and was truly local and there are not many of those kind of breweries about these days.

Below: One of the oldest shops in Barnsley, A J Roberts, Photographic on Shambles Street, had acquired the status of listed building and the premises retained that title even when the Roberts left for another site. The new owners, a heating firm, were anxious to retain the uniqueness of the old building but with a need to develop the interior to bring it more in line with their needs. During a period of controlled burning, however, things got somewhat out of hand for this firm, necessitating a call to the Borough Fire Brigade.

Here we can see the members of the brigade trying to save what they can of the property and of the other premises nearby, like the still surviving Three Travellers Inn, now called something different however, and the empty shop between which at one time was a service garage. At this time it is standing empty like the other shops and businesses on this street awaiting re-development.

Right: A sight that could have been a tragedy for many a citizen of Barnsley in 1960 was that of Eddy Burton's well known fish and chip shop at the corner of Eldon Street and Beckett Street appearing to go up in flames. The fire was caused by the dripping overheating and catching fire.

The amount of smoke that this naturally caused, especially as the shop used a gas fired range, made it seem worse than it was and it was not long before members of the Barnsley Borough Fire Brigade, with their appliances ready to save a landmark in the town, had it all under control with nothing more than smoke damage to the shop and the upstairs rooms. To the relief of the many devotees of Burton's fish and chips, the shop was able to re-open for business the following day after massive efforts to clean up the mess.

Office staff in CEAG provide the necessary business-like air a successful firm requires. The 1920s brought the demand for bulbs to give an unfailing service underground so CEAG began to produce low voltage bulbs for inclusion into its lamps and within a short time it entered a new field, alongside its mining activities, with the manufacture of low voltage bulbs for the rapidly growing motor industry. The firm suffered a serious set back in 1935 when the factory was destroyed by fire but within a year it was rebuilt and continued to prosper, During the Second World War it was involved in the production of lighting and other engineering equipment required for the fighting services.

After the war, with a greater emphasis placed on safety in the coal mining industry, CEAG became involved in producing new lamps which were more powerful and longer lasting as well as working with the automobile industry in producing the more sophisticated lamps and bulbs modern cars needed.

Above: Eldon Street contained many other names other than Burton's fish and chip shop with long associations with it. The street had come into being in about 1840 and its more famous inhabitants included Harralls 'Ring Shop' and Brown's Ironmongery business, the latter surviving until 1960. Opposite the Public Hall was the still remaining Barnsley Arcade with tobacconists, S Tetley and Son, at the

entrance to it for over forty years. The Public Hall itself has had a chequered history as though there has never been a proper function for it in the town. It has served as the School of Art, the Library and the Technical School as well as being the venue for concerts, dances, lectures and meetings. Today its grand facade and its massive 'body' dominate this end of the street in a forlorn, ornamental sort of way as though no-one wants to lose it yet no-one knows what to do with it.

Above right: A lone pit pony wearing its own safety lamp made by local firm CEAG Ltd. which had come to Barnsley in 1912. The firm became a household name immediately after the First World War in the mining circles of South Yorkshire and

beyond for the design and the manufacture of a comprehensive range of lamps for use underground and for the same range in other industries requiring low voltage portable lamps of robust construction and reliability. The industries on which Britain had based its economic success before the war were in the process of decline and textiles, iron and steel, shipbuilding and coal mining were now more vulnerable than ever to foreign competition. In those post war years, therefore, there was not only a need for them to be revitalised but for new ones to grow, hence the importance of the products which CEAG made to aid and speed production.

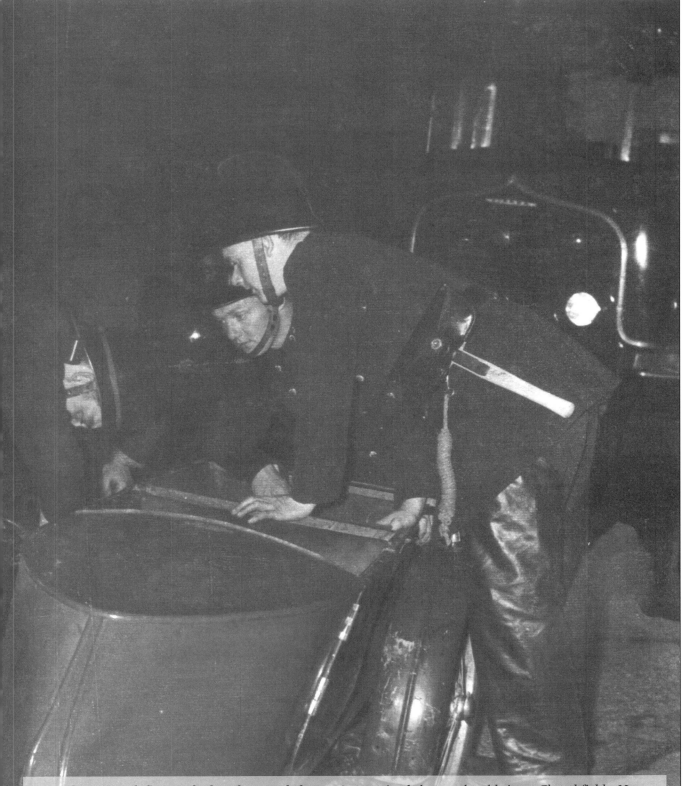

Barnsley Borough firemen look rather puzzled at the sight of a sidecar which had caught fire after an accident in Rotherham Road. Being firemen, however, nothing should surprise them as fires and accidents are not ordinary events but the result of something out of the ordinary. That sidecar looks a bit open to the weather! The brigade moved to its new Headquarters in Bradway at the beginning of the 1960s and its new neighbour was the ambulance service whereas the old ones, the police remained close to the old site at Churchfields. New station, new sophisticated equipment, same fires, however, whether it be at a glassworks in Stairfoot, above a poodle parlour in Wesley Street, sorting out the mess after a traffic accident, dealing with a smouldering hayfield, taking an active part in Civil Defence exercises, still very much in the thoughts of the nation during this 'cold war' period, or educating the young or not so young in fire prevention, the job did not change - much.

The gentleman second from the left standing with all the prizewinners at Barnsley's civic Olde English Fayre is Mr Joe Richards, then a Director of Barnsley AFC since 1920, who eventually became its chairman after the war and held such posts as President of the Football League and Selector of the National team. The England team manager in those days usually had no say in team selection! Richards began life as a miner and moved into the offices after breaking a leg; he rapidly gained promotion within the National Coal Board and then left to form his own fuel business. This allowed him the time to spend on administering the club and advance his position within the football hierarchy and for his services to football he received a knighthood. He had a reputation as chairman of keeping the club financially stable which meant he made sure the books balanced and there were no debts, selling players if that were deemed necessary, including the young Tommy Taylor.

The sad fact is that the club never achieved the success on the field that the fans desired during his eighteen years as chairman and in that great year for English football, 1966, Richards retired.